Building Your Own Theology, Volume 2
Exploring

Second Edition

Richard S. Gilbert

Also in this series:
Building Your Own Theology, Volume 1: Introduction
Building Your Own Theology, Volume 3: Ethics

Unitarian Universalist Association
Boston

Copyright © 2005 by the Unitarian Universalist Association, 24 Farnsworth Street, Boston, MA 02210-1409.

All rights reserved.

Printed in the United States

ISBN 978-1-55896-493-8

Cover designer: Kimberly Glyder

17 / 9 8 7 6 5 4

Note

Some quotations in this curriculum contain language that may be considered sexist or exclusionary. For the sake of accuracy, they have been printed here with their original wording.

"The Healing Time" reprinted by permission of Pesha Joyce Gertler. Previously published in *CrossCurrents*, *World*, *Claiming the Spirit Within*, and *Pontoon*. Set to music by Elizabeth Alexander, forthcoming on CD under title "Finally On My Way to Yes," the first line of "The Healing Time." Also published in *Healing and Empowering the Feminine*, by Sylvia Shaindel Senensky, a Canadian Jungian analyst.

Chalice extinguishing by Barbara Wells reprinted by permission of the author.

Contents

Preface		v
Introduction		ix
Preparation Materials for Session 1		xviii
Session 1	Truth and Authority: What Do We Know for Sure?	1
Session 2	Unity in Diversity: What Holds Us Together?	9
Session 3	The Nature of Spirituality: What Is Holy?	17
Session 4	Sin and Salvation: Are We Saved?	27
Session 5	Eschatology: How Do We Account for Evil?	34
Session 6	Justice and the Beloved Community: What Is Our Place in the World?	43
Session 7	Individualism and Community: What Is the Role of the Church?	50
Session 8	Suffering and Meaning: Why Do Bad Things Happen?	58
Session 9	Death and Immortality: How Do We Celebrate Life?	66
Session 10	A Spiritual Check-Up: Where Do We Go from Here?	74
Resources		77
Evaluation		81

Preface

I wrote the first volume of *Building Your Own Theology* in 1978 at the suggestion of then-UUA religious education consultant Leslie Westbrook. The impetus for this venture was my experience of many orientation sessions for people new to Unitarian Universalism at the First Unitarian Church of Rochester, New York. Typically, I invited people to speak about their religious past and why they are exploring liberal religion. Most of those participating were "come-outers" from some more traditional faith, full of theological rejection for the faith of their childhood and youth. I wanted them at least to feel like "come-inners," not simply rebelling against orthodox faith, but moving into an exciting new theological zone. It was not enough to reject the Trinity, a supernatural God, or creedalism and be able to articulate what they did not believe. I was confident that on the basis of those experiences, they could find something to affirm. And in clarifying what they could affirm they might well find building stones amidst the wreckage of their former faith. They ought not throw out the baby with the bathwater. There are fundamental and universal values that people bring with them—family relationships, religious experiences, and theological insights that ought not to be lost.

In 1977 I gathered a small group of church friends and members in the church parsonage living room and began to develop the curriculum that was to become *Building Your Own Theology.* It had to be a group experience so they could share and learn from one another. It had to be respectful of their religious past. It had to provide the tools and the building blocks for developing their own credos—which etymologically is more than "I believe." It also means "I value."

I began by developing a theological model based on the insights of people like James Fowler, Lawrence Kohlberg (and later Carol Gilligan), and Jean Piaget. I began with the assumption that all of us, no matter what our theology, need to accomplish certain theological developmental tasks and understand the interrelationships of theological concepts such as understanding of human nature, ultimate reality, ethical human relations, our relationship with the past, and religion as the quest for meaning. So I developed various learning exercises from my experience in religious education. In the revised edition of *Building Your Own Theology*, volume 1, I suggested that the Purposes and Principles of the Unitarian Universalist Association were a necessary but not sufficient condition for developing a personal theology. The process I outlined in that program was intended as a step toward creating a personal credo—a specific set of meanings, values, and convictions that inform and direct the living of one's life. Reliance on the Purposes and Principles as a substitute for being able to articulate a personal credo is inadequate for Unitarian Universalists who take their faith seriously.

Volume 2 of *Building Your Own Theology* is a continuation of the credo-development process with the introduction of other theological issues crucial for formulating a faith. As volume 1 began with an introduction to the Seven Principles of the Unitarian Universalist Association Bylaws, volume 2 begins with an introduction to the often neglected Sources in the UUA Bylaws that inform our theological endeavors and represent our religious pluralism. Each session of the program includes an essay for participants to read before meeting.

Familiarity with each essay will be important as we consider the theological issues in each session. This program has ten sessions. Of course participants can expand, add, or subtract sessions depending on their local situations and their imaginations. As always, the essays and exercises presented here are merely suggestive, and creative revisions and substitutions are encouraged. There are a number of alternative activities in each session, each within the suggested time guidelines.

The time guidelines for each activity are also merely suggestive; sessions have been designed to take ninety minutes, leaving time for breaks and making the sessions crisp. The idea is to select those activities that seem most helpful. Other activities can be used for additional sessions, in covenant groups, or in other educational settings.

The *Building Your Own Theology* program revolves around the creation of personal credos, and the homework for each session should feed directly into each participant's credo. Participants should complete this homework before each session to leave maximum group time for discussion and group activities. After one group session and before the next, participants should write or rewrite their credos in the light of what they have learned and questions that have been raised.

During the sessions participants may share parts of their credos. This should, of course, be voluntary, but it does add richness. The credo sharing can be spontaneous or prepared in advance.

Each session includes one or more alternate activities. The group may select which ones seem appropriate. Be flexible. This is a structured program but it need not be rigid. If a topic strikes sparks, by all means, stay with it.

Preparation for Leaders or Coordinators

Publicity for the program should state that participation in *Building Your Own Theology: Introduction* (volume 1) is a prerequisite, although exceptions can be made. It would be well also to state that regular attendance is expected and that a certain amount of homework between sessions will be part of the experience. *Building Your Own Theology: Exploring* (volume 2) is not a bull session on religion. It is a personal and group discipline.

Pre-registration for the program is recommended. Collect any fees at this time. Copies of the course outline (Table of Contents) and a reg-

istration form can be combined. Have a few copies of *Building Your Own Theology*, volume 1, available for sale or loan in the event members have not kept copies or wish to refresh their memories of the earlier experience. All participants will need to purchase copies of this book.

Necessary readings and worksheets for doing homework are provided before each session. Worksheets and other resources designed to be used in the session itself can be found immediately after the session. Like the first volume of *Building Your Own Theology*, this program has been designed for use by a Unitarian Universalist church or fellowship with or without professional religious leadership. The basic philosophy is the same; the format is similar. The only differences are the issues and a somewhat more flexible outline. While a background in theology or religious studies would be beneficial for the leaders, it is not required, providing they are willing to do the work of preparation. Each session is outlined as follows: Purpose, Materials, Preparation, Chalice Lighting, various activities, Homework for the next session, and the Closing Ceremony.

The leader(s) should read the entire curriculum and any of the recommended readings that interest them first. This curriculum can be led by an individual, a pair of co-leaders, or a series of group members who rotate leadership. The leader(s) should have taken *Building Your Own Theology: Introduction* if at all possible. Some familiarity with the process is very important if this course is to be successful.

Preparation for Participants

- Bring some form of notebook, preferably a three-ring binder, for note taking and materials.

- Bring your credo from *Building Your Own Theology*, volume 1 (if available), because you will be referring to and adding to it.

- Fill out the Credo Survey on page xviii (preferably before doing the reading).

- Read the Reading for Session 1 (page xxiv), Genesis 22:1-9, and "The Blind Men and the Elephant" in *From Long Ago and Many Lands* by Sophia Lyon Fahs.

- Access *www.beliefnet.com* and complete the "Belief-o-Matic" and "What's Your Spiritual Type" surveys found there. If you do not have access to the Internet, you may be able to access it through the church computer or your local library.

Introduction

The 2005 report of the UUA Commission on Appraisal explores the question of whether or not there is a theological core that holds the disparate and pluralistic movement of Unitarian Universalism together. I doubt there is any single theological position that ties us into one movement, but the radical openness with which we approach the spiritual quest is a uniting element. As historian Conrad Wright expresses it in his book *Walking Together*, what has bound this group of congregations and their people is not common belief but a covenant to walk together into the mysteries, fully respecting diversity, learning from one another, vigorously discussing the issues that confront us, and taking individual and collective action upon them. I hope this further exploration in liberal religious theology will help make our walking together not only more meaningful but also more enjoyable.

The Bylaws of the Unitarian Universalist Association inform us that "the living tradition we share draws from many sources," and after naming them, concludes, "Grateful for the religious pluralism which enriches and ennobles our faith, we are inspired to deepen our understanding and expand our vision. As free congregations we enter into this covenant, promising to one another our mutual trust and support."

1. Direct experience of that transcending mystery and wonder, affirmed in all cultures, which moves us to a renewal of the spirit and an openness to the forces that create and uphold life.

Unitarian Universalists have never been accused of being fanatics. The great jurist Oliver Wendell Holmes was asked at a dinner party what his religion was. He answered "Unitarian." "Why?" his interrogator continued. He replied, "In Boston everyone must be something, and the very least you can be is a Unitarian." Admittedly we are—to say the least—differently religious. How different are we? Are we those who, as the Muslim mystic Rumi puts it, merely "know the conventions" or those whose very "souls burn"? Or does that sound too fanatical for us?

In March of 1995 six hundred only somewhat fanatical Unitarian Universalist ministers gathered in convocation trying to define the "passionate and enduring center of our faith." Clearly this was not a business convention, a political rally, or a huge party. Whatever it was, it was powerful and a bit controversial among a number of religious humanists who found it overly mystical and even theistic. The convocation's covenant reads in part,

In the midst of mystery and the enduring presence of religious community, the creative power of transforming love engages us in the beauty and tragedy of life to awaken compassion, call us to justice and invite us to live in harmony with the earth. In light of our commitment to our Unitarian Universalist faith and our responsibility to our colleagues, congregations and the world:

We covenant to affirm that at the heart of our faith is a profound sense of the holy and a critical trust in the power of reason. We lift up this universal religious experience, while respecting our different religious languages and symbols, in worship, religious education, fellowship and service.

It concluded, "Thus do we covenant with one another and all that is holy." Are Unitarian Universalists "fanatic" in this sense? Or are we averse to transcendence? Do religious liberals have transcendent experiences that take us beyond our surface selves and remind us that we are part of something greater than ourselves—something that brings out the best in us, that transforms our lives, transcends the ordinary, gives us a glimpse into another realm of being, and makes life worth living?

Unitarian Universalists tend to be religiously cautious—not easily carried away. Writing about the results of the 1967 survey of Unitarian Universalist beliefs in his 1973 book *Religion among the Unitarian Universalists: Converts in the Stepfathers' House*, Robert Tapp finds that over three quarters of religious liberals find their membership in their congregation supports rather than transforms their previous value systems. A current survey might yield similar results. And yet much of current denominational rhetoric is full of transformation talk. The question might be raised as to whether we are open to transcendent experience enough to be transformed by it.

Are we a bit like the sometimes cynical playwright Samuel Beckett? Out for a ride with a friend on one of the most beautiful days of the year, he exclaimed "This is a marvelous day!" "It sure is," replied his friend. "It's the kind of day that makes you glad to be alive." A frown crossed Beckett's face. "Well," he said, "I wouldn't go that far."

Theologian Robert Mesle writes in words that might satisfy many Unitarian Universalists in discussing the transcendent: "I am more comfortable talking about the experience of the sacred than about the existence of a divine being."

But the nineteenth-century Transcendentalists, whom we claim as our forebears, believed in a direct experience of divinity. In one classic passage Ralph Waldo Emerson writes,

> Standing on the bare ground—my head bathed by the blithe air and uplifted into infinite space—all mean egotism vanishes. I become a transparent eyeball; I am nothing; I see all; the currents of the Universal Being circulate through me; I am part and parcel of God.

Clarke, Emerson, and Channing wrote that the nineteenth-century feminist writer Margaret Fuller had been despondent, feeling the world had no place for her, and that the church offered no spiritual comfort. Pausing beside a stream at the end of a long walk, she had a mystical experience:

> I saw there was no self; that selfishness was all folly, and the result of circumstance; that it was only because I thought the self real that I suffered; that I had only to live in the idea of the all, and all was mine. This truth came to me, and I received it unhesitatingly; so that I was for that hour taken up into God. In that true ray most of the relations of earth seemed mere films, phenomena.

2. Words and deeds of prophetic women and men which challenge us to confront powers and structures of evil with justice, compassion, and the transforming power of love.

Ralph Waldo Emerson writes that an institution is "the lengthened shadow of a man." As a noncreedal people, Unitarian Universalists tend to focus on individuals as embodiments of religion rather than on the creeds that seek to summarize religious beliefs. As Emerson puts it, "What you are thunders so loud I cannot hear what you say." These words remind us that UUs are more attuned to the words and deeds of faith-full men and women than of creedal precision.

There are times when one might think the major Unitarian Universalist holy day should be called "All Heretics Day," to indicate our heretical past. Heretical here refers not so much to doctrinal unorthodoxy as to the power of choice—from the original meaning of the Greek *harein*—to choose. These prophets of the human spirit trace a history that binds us to a powerful and varied tradition. One of our old church school texts by Rolland Emerson Wolfe was entitled *Men of Prophetic Fire* to indicate the passionate conviction of the Hebrew prophets, who form a kind of metaphor for this second of our Sources.

The Hebrew prophets believed people could take time by the forelock and shape their common future. They revealed alternatives and their consequences, thus exhibiting a faith in free will, a decisive turning point in the history of religion. They were not seers, not fortune tellers; they believed they were spokespersons for Yahweh.

These people of prophetic fire envisioned a Messianic kingdom of love, justice and peace, perhaps best expressed in the Hebrew word shalom. As Erich Fromm wrote in *You Shall Be As Gods: A Radical Interpretation of the Old Testament and Its Traditions*, "The prophets are revolutionaries who rob force and power of their moral and religious disguises." They are, in every sense of the word, redemptive rebels.

Humanity has witnessed the proud procession of the prophets, men and women of vision and courage who felt a life mission to serve, to get outside their own skin and seek a newer world. Jesus, the "prophet from Nazareth," is in their tradition, as are St. Francis of Assisi, who proclaimed love for all living creatures above the rigors of ritual religion; Mohammed, who prayed to one god of justice; and Maimonides, the twelfth-century Jewish scholar who taught the greatest charity was justice. In our own tradition we have William Ellery Channing, Theodore Parker, Susan B. Anthony, Clara Barton, and John Haynes Holmes, among a host of others.

What of the prophetic spirit today? The time has long passed when a scruffy shepherd like Amos could walk into the capitol city and begin preaching. Now he would be committed, arrested, or ignored. The social context is far different now, and the charismatic prophet has a much more difficult time securing a hearing in our mass society with its electronic communications. Now social reform is affected not so much by loners speaking from some soapbox in the public square as by groups of citizens, infused with the prophetic spirit, who still seek the Beloved Community.

There are other men and women of prophetic fire who live among us; their names are not the subject of nightly telecasts, but they are those who nonetheless live their lives for others, who drop the plumb line, who take time seriously, who seek to shape history, who find the meaning of life in the struggle for justice in community.

We look to our heroes—our prophets—as standards by which to measure ourselves. We look for embodiment in our leaders—believing they are an incarnation of the divine. We then dissect our heroes—our leaders—with a moral scalpel of exquisite sharpness, bemoaning how they have let us down. We find in their flaws an excuse to refrain from the hard work of the world.

What we perhaps can't come to admit is that for all our need of heroes, they are all flawed—every one of them. Moses was a murderer and David was an adulterer. Jesus lost his temper and tipped over tables in the temple. Martin Luther had a pornographic tongue. Thomas Jefferson fathered a child by one of his slaves. Emma Goldman had a series of sexual relationships that would make modern-day observers blanche. Franklin Delano Roosevelt had a longtime extramarital liaison with a woman who was with him the day he died at Warm Springs. John F. Kennedy is widely known to have wandered from his conjugal bed. Martin Luther King Jr. has come under intense scrutiny and has been found to be less than perfect.

We are all more human than otherwise. Each of us is a bundle of contradictions, inconsistencies, and dubious ethical behaviors. Learning that our folk heroes share finitude with us can but encourage us to meet the ambiguities of existence with the same soul searching, the same commitment to justice.

3. Wisdom from the world's religions, which inspires us in our ethical and spiritual life.

Unitarian Universalism has had an unusually intimate relationship with the great religions. In the 1568 Edict of Torda, Unitarian King John Sigismund of Transylvania decreed toleration for all the religions of his realm: Calvinists, Lutherans, Roman Catholics, Greek Orthodox, and Unitarians.

In nineteenth-century America Ralph Waldo Emerson and Theodore Parker, among others, studied Eastern religions with appreciation. William Ellery Channing, although a devout Unitarian Christian, declared himself a member of the "Universal Church" from which no one can be excommunicated save by the "death of goodness in (their) own breast." Universalist George de Benneville said, "The inner Spirit makes (us) feel that behind every appearance of diversity there is an interdependent unity of all things."

In the late nineteenth century this universalist impulse found expression in the 1867 Free Religious Association, a Transcendentalist-inspired splinter group that felt the Unitarian movement had grown beyond Christianity, from the faith of the soul's childhood to "universal religion," "the faith of the soul's manhood." While the Free Religious Association languished, its spirit paved the way for the 1893 World Parliament of Religions and the formation of the International Association of Religious Freedom in 1900, linking the liberal branches of major world faiths.

The Unitarian Universalist Association's 1999 Statement of Conscience, "Beyond Religious Tolerance: The Challenges of Interfaith Cooperation Begin with Us," reaffirmed our Unitarian Universalist commitment to more than tolerance of the world's religions. It encourages us to respect and learn from these great living faiths. *Tolerance* can be a condescending term with its implication that diverse views are allowed to exist from a spiritually superior point of view. *Respect* implies recognition of the validity of each of humanity's ways of being religious.

However, such respect can lead to *syncretism*, the amalgamation of the values of each faith in a single worldwide religious perspective. In the vernacular, this could mean merely a kind of cafeteria creed, a pot-luck profession of faith in which the world's religions are laid out on some great table while we simply walk along with our trays taking a little bit of this and a little bit of that for our sustenance. Is such a universal religion possible or even desirable? Is a faith for the global village a defensible religious position? Can such a faith contribute to religious meaning?

This universal religion stands as a protest against all parochialism, against all pretense that there is one true faith, against all monopolistic religious claims to ultimacy. Faith for the global village undercuts the supremacy of revealed religions and the big bang theory of religious development—that God revealed the truth in a particular time and place.

But is what we seek a *one-world faith*, as if we could construct a single religious movement for all humanity? Or is it a *faith for one world*, a faith for the global village that is radically open to the varied strands of human experience? Or do we seek a religious viewpoint adequate to the social reality of the one world in which we all live? Clearly the world is too dangerous for provincialism, nationalism, and ethnocentrism. The world is too small for anything but true universalism. But how can we achieve this within a single faith tradition?

It seems almost mean to critique such a lofty religious ideal, but universal religion lays itself wide open. It can become simply a "cut and paste" proposition, in which we snip out a story here, a symbol there, and fashion them into some eclectic theological montage. We are apt to forget that religious experience grows out of particular cultures, in specific times and places; it must have the smell of our own ground.

Shouldn't we seek a radical openness to the values of the many faiths of the global village?

How large a circle can we belong to meaningfully? We cannot meaningfully create a single world faith, nor ought we to try. We can cherish and teach those universal truths taught by all the great prophets of humanity and we can penetrate our own faith to find common ground with those who have penetrated their own, sharing the archetypes of human experience.

4. Jewish and Christian teachings that call us to respond to God's love by loving our neighbors as ourselves.

Jews are the people of the book. While these religious writings are not an accurate or objective history of the Hebrew people, they do bear truth about their struggle to understand human nature and its relation to ultimate reality. These books, commonly but condescendingly known as the Old Testament, are *tendenzshrift*, history with a purpose. That is, their purpose is more religious than historical—more to persuade Jews of their unique covenant with Yahweh than to transcribe a factual history for twenty-first-century readers. These writings are *heiligeschichte*, holy history, intended to describe the way they believe God acted toward them and how they responded.

The central theme of Judaism is a covenant with God. Here we come to the "chosen people" concept—a troublesome one. Many think the Jews' concept of themselves as God's chosen people is religious arrogance of the highest order. A deeper exploration of the concept, however, reveals that Jews believe God chooses them not for special blessing but for special responsibility. If they love God, they will follow the commandments and God will love them. If not, all hell will break loose—and it did. The covenant is a mutual promise; both parties have obligations.

The Hebrew prophets took time seriously. God was not only the creator of the natural world but also Lord of history. They viewed history in linear rather than cyclical terms. In this way they had something in common with many Eastern religions, in which the thrust is to escape from historically conditioned reality. Human beings are not creatures to be pushed around by history. We are creatures who can not only respond to it but create it as well.

The prophets were not so much predictors of the future as they were its shapers. They applied an ethical standard Israel and found her wanting.

They ministered not so much to individual people as to the social structures that oppressed them. They found spiritual experience mediated by the socio-political dimensions of their time. Their concept of messianic time was horizontal, a blessed age to be ushered in by human cooperation with the Lord of history, not the second coming of Christianity's Messiah, which would be brought about by the grace of God alone.

Salvation for the prophets was more social than personal. The individual exists in community; the fate of the person is inextricably bound up in the fate of the social organism. This teaching inspired Unitarian Universalist minister John Haynes Holmes to write of his church,

> The community church is an institution of religion dedicated to the service of humanity. . . . It substitutes for the individual the social group as an object of salvation. It interprets religion in terms of social reconstruction, and dedicates its members to the fulfillment of social idealism. . . . the core of its faith, as the purpose of its life, is the Beloved Community.

Unitarian Universalists have been ambivalent about their Jewish and Christian heritage. At a joint meeting of the Universalist Church of America and the American Unitarian Association in Syracuse, New York, in 1959, the two denominations debated whether Jesus should be included in the statement of purposes of the yet-to-be created Unitarian Universalist Association. It was the Council of Nicea all over again, with the prophet from Nazareth at the center of the controversy. On the one hand, including Jesus would recognize the roots from which we had come; he was after all the religious hero of our Christian heritage.

On the other hand, what of Jews who might wish to join us? Would Jesus be a stumbling block? And what of those from other religious traditions? Would they resent naming this one prophet to the exclusion of all others? The issue was joined; passions ran high, but compromise prevailed. Jesus was dropped, but in his place were inserted the words "to cherish and spread the universal truths taught by the great prophets and teachers of humanity in every age and tradition, immemorially summarized in the Judeo-Christian tradition as love to God and love to man."

Here was an example of how the democratic method writes ecclesiastical theology. No one was completely happy, and a few were unutterably angry. All were witnesses of the audacious attempt to write theology by a committee-of-the-whole. Democracy, one might conclude, paraphrasing Winston Churchill, is the worst form of church governance except for every other. Yet our forebears cherished the original ethical and spiritual teachings of Jesus as central to their faith. When the religion about Jesus was planted in the creeds of Christendom, heretics began to bloom. As the Christian Church went on to great things—to become the religion of the empire—it lost something of that initial appeal. Still, such heretics as the sixteenth-century Michael Servetus of Spain and nineteenth-century salvationist James Relley of England clearly thought of themselves as Christian, as did William Ellery Channing, who urged the nineteenth-century American Unitarians to stay within the standing order of Congregational Churches. It was not until the advent of the Free Religious Association in 1867, of which Ralph Waldo Emerson was the first member, and the *Humanist Manifesto* of 1933, signed by many UU ministers, that it became possible to be a Unitarian or Universalist without also being a Christian.

Twice in the 1940s the Universalist Church was denied membership in what became the National Council of Churches because it was not Christian enough. In 1957 the American Unitarian Association journal, *The Christian Register*, became *The Unitarian Register*. In the 2000 *Fulfilling the Promise* survey of theological beliefs, we find that approximately 10 percent of UUs considered themselves Christian at that time.

Currently we can say the denomination is officially neither Christian nor non-Christian. There are churches that are expressly Christian and those that are expressly not, while most would not presume a position on the issue. It is abundantly clear that many in our midst consider themselves liberal Christians.

The Unitarian Universalist Christian and those who see themselves as children of that tradition embrace the ethical strength of liberal Christianity. Christian ethics constitute a perennial attack on self-aggrandizement and narcissism; here is a faith that stands unashamedly for sacrifice and altruism in a selfish world. The cross could symbolize the "I" crossed out. The demands of the Biblical God are unyielding and do not admit to the cultural relativism and wishy-washy liberalism with which our movement is charged. The long-standing joke that God did not give us the Ten Commandments but the Ten Suggestions is more than humor; it is a telling commentary. Unitarian Universalist Christianity chastises the movement for lack of theological substance.

The Christian Gospel does not exist to make us comfortable in our souls but daring in our spirits. Read seriously, the Bible is a radical book whose ethical precepts stretch us beyond ourselves. As Thoreau says of the Bible,

> I know of no book that has so few readers. There is none so truly strange, and heretical, and unpopular . . . There are, indeed, severe things in it that no man should read aloud more than once. "Seek first the kingdom of Heaven." "Lay not up for yourself treasures on earth." "If thou wilt be perfect, go and sell that thou hast, and give to the poor, and thou shalt have treasure in heaven." "For what is a man profited, if he shall gain the whole world, and lose his own soul?"

Liberal Christianity is a powerful force among us because it provides a coherent and articulate perspective and a consistent theological and liturgical language. Literalists among us belittle the archaic pre-scientific language of the Bible with its three-tiered universe of heaven, earth, and hell. But the Bible was never intended to be a book of science or history—it is a fundamentally religious book, full of evocative poetry, powerful symbols, and captivating myths that cut beneath the surface of our lives to the life of the spirit beneath.

Try to understand Western culture without the Jewish/Christian Bible. Music, art, and literature all owe a great debt to it. Biblical poetry, if not unsurpassed, is at least on a par with anything the human race has written. The majesty of the Psalms, the homely wisdom of Proverbs, the insights of Job, the drama of the Gospels, and the poetry of Paul. Where would we be without them? Our very consciousness has been shaped by this language, however ancient it may be.

We cannot be religious in general. We need the specificity of language; we need to know our roots even before we can reject them. Religious liberals are charged with intellectual amnesia and spiritual myopia in cutting themselves off from what might sustain them. The danger is not that we have outgrown our Christian heritage but that it will outgrow us. And so many find comfort in saying these familiar words: "In the love of truth and in the spirit of Jesus, we unite for the worship of God and the service of humanity."

Of course there are perils in trying to modernize Jesus. We attempt to take a first-century agrarian ethic and force it into the procrustean bed of twenty-first-century global problems. And there are exemplars equally as noble: Buddha, who forsook wealth and power to help others seek enlightenment; Socrates, whose relentless pursuit of truth led to martyrdom; and other prophets of every age and tradition. Veneration of Jesus can come very close to idolatry. Does this place too much confidence in a figure about whom we know barely enough to write a decent obituary?

And can—should—the cross be our ultimate religious symbol? Howard Thurman, the late and great black preacher, once remarked that he never had a cross in his church because it reminded him not of Jesus but of the Ku Klux Klan. The cross is a powerful symbol of sacrificial death and the triumph of the human spirit over bestial cruelty. Pain and suffering are inherent in life but they are not all of life. Does the cross leave out of life that which should be celebrated? After all, Channing compares it to God's "erecting a gallows in the center of the universe." He goes on to say, "Do not feel as if Christianity has spoken the last word. It is the characteristic of the divine truth that it is infinitely fruitful." And the iconoclast Emerson writes, "Attach not thyself to the Christian symbol, but to the moral sentiment which carries innumerable Christianities, humanities and divinities in its bosom."

5. Humanist teachings, which counsel us to heed the guidance of reason and the results of science, and warn us against idolatries of the mind and spirit.

Religious humanism is something old and something new, something borrowed and something true. It is as old as the Greek philosopher Protagoras who says, "As for the gods, I do not know whether they exist or not. Life is too short for such difficult enquiries . . . . Man is the measure of all things, determining what does and does not exist."

Humanism is as old as Buddhism, Confucianism, and Taoism, nontheistic faiths all. It has a noble history in such figures as Socrates and other ancient philosophers. The poet Shelley writes, "Ah! What a divine religion might be found out if charity were really made the principle of it, instead of faith."

It lives in Alexander Pope's familiar words, "Know then thyself. Presume not God to scan, the proper study of mankind is man." And also in the thoughts of the nineteenth-century reformer Robert Ingersoll: "Justice is the only worship, love is the only priest, ignorance is the only slavery, happiness is the only good; the time to be happy is now; the place to be happy is here. The way to be happy is to make others so."

Religious humanism is as new as twentieth-century Unitarian Universalists seeking to be differently religious before the rising tide of religious fundamentalism. It is as new as the Humanist Manifesto I from the 1930s, Humanist Manifesto II from the 1970s, and Humanist Manifesto III for the new millennium.

Religious humanism is something borrowed. It stems primarily from Greek and Roman philosophers, with a touch of the Renaissance and the Enlightenment, mixed with a generous dose of the scientific revolution and modernized by humanistic psychology. In its more recent incarnations, it is a reaction against traditional Christianity and theological theism, an affirmation that religion is not limited to theistic experience.

Religious humanism is something true. Its essence is perhaps summed up in the words "we are the meaning makers." We are *homo religiosus*, creatures who must have meaning. For many, that meaning is inherent in the cosmos, built into the structures of being by God. For religious humanists, however, meaning is not so much discovered as created out of the raw stuff of our own experience, the interplay of self with community and nature and history. To religious humanists divine revelation is but human knowledge projected on a cosmic screen; the will of God is the projection of human needs on a divine—imaginary—screen. For the religious humanist, the human task is to discover meaning through reason and reflection on experience.

Albert Camus succinctly summarizes the essence of humanism:

I continue to believe that this world has no ultimate meaning. But I know that something in it has a meaning and that is man, because he is the only creature to insist on having one.

This world has at least the truth of man, and our task is to provide its justification against fate itself . . . If, after all men cannot always make history have a meaning, they can always act so that their own lives have one.

The religious humanist believes that while we cannot do very much about the Ultimate, we can do something about how we respond to it, how we live our lives in the proximate world. We are forced back upon ourselves for whatever meaning there is in existence. Finding that life is cosmically absurd is not the end of religion but the beginning of the creation of human meaning.

Religious humanism should never be equated with atheism. It does not subscribe to H. L. Mencken's definition of faith as "an illogical belief in the occurrence of the improbable." Atheism rejects deity but puts nothing in its place. The atheist must move beyond atheism or be nothing but a nihilist, believing in nothing. The religious humanist does not deify humanity but recognizes, for better or for worse, his or her fate will be determined with other human beings.

Most religious humanists acknowledge an ultimate reality behind all things, yet this belief often takes the form of a deeply reverent agnosticism before the Mysterium Tremendum and an awed silence before the cosmic creativity. Some humanists are, in short, "ecstatic humanists," retaining that pragmatic humanism that subscribes to the Russian proverb "Pray to God but row for the shore."

Would religious humanism, as an open-minded, creatively evolving, anthropocentric faith, have the kind of spiritual stamina to resist evil? The alleged arrogance of humanism, its easy historical optimism, and its calm confidence in the inherent virtue of human nature are under siege.

Furthermore, religious humanism has at times been marked by an arid rationalism. Does it have the capacity to sing and soar? Where is the humanist inspiration to help us face the lions of the twenty-first century? Where is its Twenty-third Psalm to comfort the afflicted? Can religious humanism, an optimistic faith, give hope when we are confronted by defeat, suffering, and death? Can religious humanism sustain us when we stand poised at the edge of life and death?

Reason, while an indispensable part of our religious tool kit, is not omni-competent. Is reason simply another mode of feeling? Are there dimensions of the human predicament with which reason cannot fully cope? Is then reason a necessary but not sufficient condition for deep religion, which is rationality and feeling, will and spirit? Does reason, the mainstay of humanism, have room for tragedy?

There is a time for doubt, uncertainty, and ambiguity. But preoccupation with them is not a very satisfying way to spend a life. There must also be a time for faith in the worthwhileness of life. There must be a time for decisive action even in the face of uncertainty. There must be a time for emphatic convictions even in the face of ambiguity.

Theologian Leonard Sweet writes about the need for a core of central values that does not change very much and the need for explorations at the growing edges of the spirit. He likened the process to that of cave explorers who tie one end of a rope to an object outside before exploring unknown caverns. As they grope their way through the maze of passageways, they unwind the rope. This is a powerful and intriguing image for religious liberals who so properly eschew theological orthodoxies and dogmatic certainties. Don't we need a core of convictions that changes only very slowly in the light of the most profoundly moving experiences? And at the same time, don't we need a growing edge to explore new passageways of the spirit? Religious humanism would answer in the affirmative.

6. Spiritual teachings of Earth-centered traditions which celebrate the sacred circle of life and instruct us to live in harmony with the rhythms of nature.

The addition of this sixth Source by vote of the 1995 General Assembly was a matter of some controversy among Unitarian Universalists—whether it should be included as one of the religious sources that sustains us. That seems strange in view of the fact that all the great religions have been at least partly based in the natural world—in pagan worldviews. Several of the great festivals of Judaism and Christianity are derived from pagan sources. Sukkoth, the festival of booths, is a harvest festival. The dating of Christmas and Easter are hardly accidental; their placement on the calendar corresponds with popular pagan festivals in the ancient Roman world. In today's industrial and urban society, it is perhaps all the more important to affirm and celebrate the pagan in all of us.

Nigel Pennick, author of *The Pagan Book of Days*, writes,

The pagan tradition is grounded in mystical and numinous elements existing between matter and spirit. The world over it is called something like 'the old religion,' or 'the elder faith,' acknowledging its senior status among religions. It places emphasis on the links between people, their land, and the natural cycles of the seasons. In industrialized countries this connection is almost lost, because many people no longer feel rooted in the soil or connected to the seasons. In contrast, Pagan myth and ritual embody a profound respect for the physical world and the seasonal nature of the sacred year. In the pagan sacramental vision, to live according to the natural year is to be in harmony with all things natural and supernatural. The elder faith is based on the joyful celebration of life itself.

What is the relationship of liberal religion to historic paganism? The Transcendentalist movement of the nineteenth century was heavily focused on the role of the natural world order in religion. In his essay on "Nature," Ralph Waldo Emerson writes,

Why should not we also enjoy an original relation to the universe? . . . . Embosomed for a season in nature, whose floods of life stream around and through us and invite us by the powers they supply to action proportioned to nature, why should we grope among the dry bones of the past or put the living generation into masquerade out of its faded wardrobe? The sun shines today also. There is more wool and flax in the fields. There are new lands, new men, new thoughts. Let us demand our own works and laws in worship.

Henry David Thoreau went to the woods

to live deliberately, to front only the essential facts of life, to see if I could not learn what it had to teach, and not when I came to die, discover that I had not lived . . . to live deep and suck out all the marrow of life . . . . to drive life into a corner and reduce it to its lowest terms; for most men, it appears to me, are in a strange uncertainty about it, whether it is of the devil or of God, and have somewhat hastily concluded that it is the chief end of man here to glorify God and enjoy Him forever.

He says elsewhere, "Our hymn books resound with a melodious cursing of God and enduring Him forever."

Thoreau, a pagan at heart, is one of our most profound religious mentors. The fact that he withdrew from the Unitarian church in Cambridge, Massachusetts, makes him no less one of our prophets. He intertwined nature and religion to suggest that no religion worthy of the name does not base itself in the natural world. One of the supreme dangers of our time is our mistaken attempt to make a distinction between nature and humanity, as if we were not inextricably mixed up with nature. Our problem is, as Thoreau puts it, "Am I not leaves and vegetable mould myself?"

Contemporary rituals like the Water Ceremony, originally written by Lucile Longview and Carolyn McDade, call upon the power of the earth to sustain humanity. Though many variations exist, the central element is worshipers bringing symbolic portions of water from places that hold meaning for them. Many congregations begin the church year with this ingathering ceremony.

Elizabeth Fisher writes of the Spirit as it relates to nature in three ways:

First, Spirit is a dynamic essence present in all that exists. . . . Second, natural processes teach us the ways of the Spirit. This cycling of birth, life, completion and renewal, named the sacred circle of life in the sixth source, is a dynamic process, active on all levels of our experience, not just in the physical world. It applies to the continual undulating rhythms of activity available from birth to death and, for many, beyond death. . . . Third, all individuals can come to know Spirit through direct personal experience, not dogma or dictates.

Such a theology, she contends, values "all elements and beings in the natural world, and their interconnection, which creates an ethos of just and empathetic behavior." She further holds that such a view refuses to accept pain and suffering as a necessity and encourages efforts to eliminate "human produced suffering." Finally, she believes that Unitarian Universalist pagans "revere nature as a home rather than seeing the natural world as an adversary."

The eternal rhythms of nature are sustenance to our capricious humanity. Through fire and flood, through war and peace, through life and death, our little globe spins on, encircling our mother star, carrying us with it. The earth abides forever. "The voice of nature is always encouraging," writes Thoreau. When life is too much with us, when circumstance has driven us into the corner, nature's ministry works its healing: "Nature doth heal every wound. . . . It is as if I always met in those places some grand, serene, immortal, infinitely encouraging, though invisible, companion and walked with him."

Nature helps keep us humble. If we read her well, we realize how little she depends upon us and how much we depend upon her. Only recently have we begun to understand the fragility of the world in which we live and how careless we have been. One who is humble with earth does not lightly take its treasure. Even now the whole Earth groans under our technological boot. Thoreau personifies the things of earth, reminding us again and again, "What is man but a mass of thawing clay?"

Nature inspires so much of the beauty we create. Think of Van Gogh's *Sunflowers* or *Starry Night*. Consider the music that has attempted to capture the sound of the sea (Debussy's *La Mer*), or the morning ("Dawn" in the *Peer Gynt Suite* or the *Four Seasons* by Vivaldi). Remember Tennyson's *Flower in a Crannied Wall* or Blake's assertion that "if the doors of perception were cleansed, everything would appear to man as it is, infinite."

There are, of course, dangers in any of these spiritual sources. The "blood and soil" motto of Nazi Germany reminds us that even the most evil of movements can articulate some basis in the earth. James Luther Adams reminds us that religion cannot be based in the earth alone; it must have historical content lest it be socially irrelevant. It is likewise important that pagan celebrants be in the midst of the congregation, not at its periphery, for these festivals are too important to be denied to the whole people.

There is something of the pagan in us all—something that responds to the great spinning Earth that calls us to worship daily, that fills our soul, that heals our spirit, that enables us to greet the new day and the new season not with dread but with anticipation.

WORKSHEET 1

CREDO SURVEY

1. My authorities for religious truth are . . . (rank those that apply by order of importance)

    _____ church tradition

    _____ reason

    _____ divine revelation

    _____ science

    _____ nature

    _____ religious scriptures

    Which? _____

    _____ intuition

    _____ religious community

    _____ personal experience

    _____ other

    Explain.

2. Is our theological diversity a source of religious strength or weakness?
   Why?

3. Spirituality for me means . . . . (rank in order of importance)

    _____ invisible powers that sustain me

    _____ the ineffable in which I live and move and have my being

    _____ something that defies definition

    _____ an ecstatic relationship with the cosmos

    _____ a personal reservoir that sustains me

_____ an intense sense of connectedness with my neighbors near and far

_____ other

Explain.

4. The "holy" for me is . . . . (rank those that apply by order of importance)

_____ humanity

_____ history

_____ God

_____ evolution

_____ Earth

_____ process

_____ people

_____ time

_____ the cosmos

_____ other

Explain.

5. For me, *sin* means . . . . (check one)

_____ ignorance

_____ self-effacement

_____ pride

_____ attachment to the world

_____ separation from "the ground of being"

_____ missing the mark

_____ denying the unity of mind, body, and spirit

_____ victory of the id over the ego and the superego

_____ The term is meaningless to me

_____ other

Explain.

6. To me, *salvation* is achieved by . . . (check one)

_____ faith

_____ realization of one's potential

_____ character

_____ good works

_____ health or wholeness

_____ universal salvation

_____ community

_____ The term is meaningless to me.

_____ other

Explain.

7. Do you agree or disagree with the following statement? "There is a power that works in history through humanity, transforming evil into good."

Why?

8. Do you agree or disagree with the following statement? "There has been progress in the history of human civilization."

   Why?

9. If you agree with the above statement, check the three strongest supports for that belief.

   _____ growth of science and knowledge

   _____ increase in human rationality

   _____ increase of leisure time

   _____ increase in moral sensitivity

   _____ emergence of a world community

   _____ elimination of poverty and disease

   _____ other

   Explain.

10. Do you agree or disagree with the following statement? "Our potential for good can overcome our potential for evil."

    Why?

11. Albert Schweitzer once said, "Good fortune obligates," meaning that those blessed with relative comfort and prosperity have a moral obligation to "change the world." How do you react to that assertion?

_____ emphatically agree

_____ agree

_____ disagree

_____ emphatically disagree

_____ don't understand

_____ other

12. What percentage of your time, energy, and financial resources do you believe you should invest in changing the world? Circle one in each line.

| time and energy | 0 | 20% | 40% | 60% | 80% | 100% | |
| financial resources | 0 | 2% | 4% | 6% | 8% | 10% | over 10% |

13. Listed below are some understandings of the role of the liberal church. Please indicate what you feel they ought to be: very important (VI); somewhat important (SI); or not important (NI).

_____ public worship

_____ a sense of community

_____ religious education

_____ personal growth

_____ community outreach

_____ celebrating common values

_____ personal support

_____ social responsibility

14. Which statement below best expresses your understanding of the meaning of human suffering?

_____ God sends suffering to test us. If we are worthy, we endure suffering and are assured eternal bliss.

_____ God sends suffering because we have been evil. God withholds suffering if we are good.

_____ Suffering comes to us from an indifferent universe of cause and effect. We can do nothing but accept that reality.

_____ Suffering can and ought to be greatly reduced in our world. Our task is to so order the world that human suffering will be virtually eliminated.

_____ Suffering is an inherent part of the human condition and an essential source of life meaning. How we deal with inevitable suffering is one of the ways we find meaning in our lives.

15. Which of the following statements best describes how you believe death fits into the human condition?

_____ Death is simply a part of life to be accepted as best we can.

_____ Death is a limit placed on us by the universe. We can extend our longevity.

_____ Death is a biological necessity in the evolutionary process.

_____ Death is merely a transitory state in the great scheme of things.

_____ Other

Explain.

16. Which of the following statements best expresses your view of immortality? (Rank those that apply in order of importance.)

_____ Immortality is a theological concept referring to heaven and hell as our destination after death.

_____ Immortality is a biological concept in which we live on through our progeny.

_____ Immortality is a historical concept in which our lives influence others over time.

_____ Immortality is a creative concept in which what beauty or truth we may have created lives on after our death.

_____ Immortality is an experiential concept in which we experience the eternal in transcendent living moments.

_____ Immortality is a state of psychic bliss.

_____ Immortality is part of a cycle of reincarnation.

_____ Other

Explain.

READING FOR SESSION 1

We begin our exploration of truth and authority with this excerpt from *The Star Gazer* by Hungarian novelist, Zsolt de Harsanyi. Galileo wrestles with his friend Cremonini over their understanding of the truth.

"Listen, Galileo," said Cremonini, "The science of the world was built on the pillars of Aristotelian wisdom. For two thousand years men have lived and died in the belief that the earth is the center of the universe and man the Lord of it. All that we know today, from logic to medicine, from botany to astronomy, is Christian and Aristotelian. A glorious structure of the human mind, every stone of which fits perfectly into the others. The greatest minds for 2000 years have worked upon it, till they have made it a perfect and splendid whole. My life has been spent in the service and admiration of this structure. Learning and teaching have brought me peace and happiness. Now I'm an old man with little time left. Tell me, why are you so cruel as to want to shake my belief in all that I love? Why do you want to poison my few last years with doubt and conflict? Leave me my peace of mind: I refuse to look into that tube!"

"But Cremonini," said Galileo, "the truth, the truth—doesn't that mean anything?"

But the trembling Cremonini still fought him off. "No, I need my peace and happiness!"

"I understand," said Galileo, "How strange! To me peace and happiness have always meant one thing: to seek truth and admit what I found. I suppose that really the whole world consists of us two, Caesare—of Cremoninis and Galileos. You keep the world back, we urge it forward. You're afraid to look at the sky because you may see there something which disproves the teaching of your whole life. I understand. Our task is heavy. And, unfortunately, there are many like you . . . *but it's only we who can triumph.*"

Cremonini countered: "And even if you do manage to prove that our earth is only a miserable little star like thousands of others, and that mankind is only a multitude of chance creatures on one of these stars? Do you really want to do that? Do you want to abase man, made in God's image, to a wretched worm? Is that what you and Copernicus and Kepler want? Is that the true purpose of astronomy?" A long silence—

"I never thought of that," Galileo answered. "I seek the truth only because I'm a mathematician, and I believe that whoever admits truth is nearer to God than those who build up their human dignity on senseless errors. And I shall go on. I must continue my path. God bless you, Caesare."

Cremonini responded: "And God keep you. *And I stay where I am!*"

Those two, who see the world so differently, stand hesitant, unable to take leave; they face each other and suddenly embrace. Their friendship has transcended their philosophical differences.

We religious liberals, in our creedless approach to truth, confess we are not always sure. The Truth eludes us. Generally we say we affirm belief "in the authority of truth known or to be known" as it was stated in the 1935 Universalist Church of America's Avowal of Faith.

One Sunday after a sermon on truth and authority entitled, "Honk If You're Not Sure," a congregant presented her minister a hand-made bumper sticker with those words.

By what authority do we claim Truth or truths? Traditionally the authority in the Western tradition has been ecclesiastical; churches have evolved creeds that purport to be the essence and sum of religious truth. Truth has also been understood to come directly from God through revelation or sacred scriptures. Historically, we have been "heretics." (*Heresy* means "to choose.") Many of us have argued that this kind of revelatory truth claim is merely a projection of personal preference on a cosmic screen.

Our liberal religious tradition has placed great emphasis on reason in religion, regarding thought processes, logic, and rational reflection as the road to religious truth. Many among us hold applying the scientific method to the religious quest in high esteem. However, it seems to some that there are truths about human existence that cannot be reduced to objective categories. Ralph Waldo Emerson reacted against these claims, positing human intuition, the individual's direct apprehension of the divine, as the surest road to truth. He protested against the "icehouse" or "morgue" of nineteenth-century Unitarianism and said we must "convert life into truth."

More recently, practioners of experiential theology have developed a more existential approach to religious truth. That is, truth is more a function of what we have learned from our experience than of what we have inherited from tradition or can learn by rational processes. They ask, "What is true for you?" Others among us say that truth seeking is a process grounded in the community and that we are, like Protagoras, the measure—or to be more accurate, the measurer—of all things. We are co-creators of religious truth that we discover in community.

In a time when today's scientific truth becomes tomorrow's quaint mythology, when the global village brings multiple perspectives into communication, and when major world religions clash openly about moral issues, the nature of truth and how we arrive at it are crucial issues.

Galileo faced up to this issue as he confronted the power of the papacy. As a scientist he was compelled to tell the truth as he discovered it; as a religionist he knew his science undermined the comforting religious assertions of the day. The Biblical God created humanity and placed it on a globe at the center of the universe—supposedly to be admired as the chief of creatures. The heresy that our earth and its inhabitants were peripheral was a mighty challenge to the "truth" of the Biblical message. It could not be allowed to stand, but in this case it triumphed. Only in 1992 did the Roman Catholic Church officially pardon Galileo for his heresy

We are truth-seeking animals, tortured by our passion for certainty, tormented by the many truth claims about us; tempted to take the easy way out—to simply buy into someone else's truth, to refuse to look into Galileo's telescope. It requires courage to resist seduction by those who would relieve our anxiety about the truth. We are competing religiously with those who presume to know it already. It takes courage to admit that sometimes we do not know for sure. Would we know a truth if we saw one?

Unitarian Universalist theologian James Luther Adams tells a delightful story about the Unitarian Universalist church school teacher who had a rabbit in class. Naturally, the subject of whether it was a girl or a boy rabbit came up. Finally, after some discussion, the teacher said, "I'll tell you what we can do. Let's take a vote." Is truth nothing more than consensus? Is it nothing more than what I feel it to be? Is it nothing more than the results of a lab experiment? Unitarian Universalists have a hard time coming to grips with truth and the authority for claiming to have found it. Some would suggest there may be no ultimate truth and that even if there were, nobody could find it. By what authority do we speak?

Unitarian Universalist theologian William Jones is instructive here. He points to a maxim of the Greek sophist Protagoras: "Man is the measure of all things." We might modify that axiom to read, "People are the measurers of all things." To say we are the measure of all things is to elevate finite humanity to the status of divinity. It would be idolatry to deify humanity by claiming we are the cosmic ultimate. However, we do claim that we are the measurers of all things, the final arbiters of values, the final judges of human meaning, the determiners of right and wrong. Not only are we the measurers of all things, we must be. This is not an assertion of human arrogance but an admission of human finitude. We are the ultimate seat of authority. It is through our sunglasses that the brilliant and often blinding truth of the cosmos is perceived. Furthermore, human nature is such that these sunglasses are permanent; we cannot remove them. An analogy is in order here: A decree of the Supreme Court is ultimate and final in the sense that it is not subject to appeal. However, the court is an interpreter of the Constitution, not its creator.

We did not create the order of things—the Earth, the moon, the stars and galaxies, photons and electrons, the evolutionary web that spun us into existence. However, we are the interpreters of this reality; we try to make some sense of it all. We seek to wrest meaning from the Earth we have inherited. While astronomically we are negligible in the cosmos, astronomically speaking, we are the astronomers.

Jones tells the Genesis story of Abraham and Isaac to dramatize the point. Abraham has been commanded, presumably by Yahweh, to take Isaac into the wilderness and slay him as a sacrifice. At the last moment a voice intervenes and tells Abraham not to slay his beloved son. How does Abraham know if the voice is that of Yahweh or of Moloch, the deity who demands human sacrifice? Abraham cannot look elsewhere for authority; he must make the final decision. As Jean Paul Sartre says, "Even if I think it is God that I obey, it is I who decided it was God who spoke to me."

But there are a few truth propositions that enable us to accept our predicament. We increasingly come to trust our own experience. No longer must we proof-text all our conclusions by reference to some holy text (secular or sacred) or some heroic guru. We honor the accumulated wisdom that inheres in the world's scriptures and in the prophets of the human spirit. But we have the task of grasping whatever slivers of truth they have chipped from the tree of knowledge.

Truth seeking is best done in community. Of course, there is no substitute for one human being thinking about, feeling, and measuring life. No one can do it for us. But there is genius in a community of individual souls who are willing and eager to share their being, thinking, feeling and measuring with others. Most of us cherish being part of a congregation with whom we can speak about the great mysteries and meanings of life. Truth emerges from a community of inquiry and dialogue. For this community, religious values are not "dead truths embalmed for posterity" but living "candidates for truth," as Ralph Waldo Emerson suggests. We have learned that revelation is not sealed in the ancient words of a self-disclosing deity; the revelation of truth is continuous. Our truths are not imprisoned in creeds but are ideas out on probation. We do not say, "Come, we have found the truth and would pass it on to you" but "Come, we seek truth and welcome you to our quest."

Perhaps it could be said that we have learned to have the courage of our confusions. When we are asked by some young truth-seeker if there is life after death, if we will avoid nuclear holocaust, if kindness in the world is on the rise—we will not be embarrassed to say simply, "I don't know." And so we live somewhere between "ecstatic confidence and despairing doubt." Somewhere between the courage of our confusions and the vacillations of our certainties we take our bearing.

In a time when our uncertainties are challenged by those who would relieve our anxiety about the truth, when there are many who would unburden us of our creative insecurities, when unquestionable answers to unanswerable questions are flung at us, we may attach our figurative bumper sticker, "Honk if you're not sure," to our truth-seeking vehicle.

But how do we seek truth? The nineteenth-century Unitarian Henry David Thoreau says, "It takes two to speak the truth—one to speak and one to hear." Our movement began as a rejection of the creeds and dogmas of the orthodox Christian Church in both Catholic and Protestant forms. In modern times we have developed two formulations that express this attitude toward truth. In the Universalist Avowal of Faith we affirm our faith in "the authority of truth known or to be known." This is a heuristic conception of truth: We hold a belief tentatively until we can confirm it or until it helps us discover something more truthful. We can act with conviction even without absolute certainty; we can be sure without being cocksure. We are not absolutely positive that we shall be alive tomorrow, but it seems a reasonably good hypothesis to act upon. This faith in existence is clearly a risk, but one that seems worth taking. We fashion our faith out of the workshop of doubt. As Gordon Allport tells us, we need to act as if there will be a tomorrow.

We might say that growth is the root metaphor of Unitarian Universalism. We are imperfect beings in the process of becoming more human—spiritually, emotionally, intellectually, and behaviorally. We seek to experience a creative surge of the spirit. Spiritually, we grow or die. While preaching an old sermon written many years before, Ralph Waldo Emerson reportedly stopped suddenly in the middle of it and said to the congregation, "The sentence which I have just read I do not now believe." One might be tempted to criticize Mr. Emerson for poor sermon preparation. If he had only reviewed it ahead of time, he might have been able to catch his change of mind in private rather than having to admit it in public. Be that as it may, the key element in this episode is that religious growth is an integral part of religion. Emerson was unashamed to admit he had changed his mind, in other words, he had grown.

Our current Unitarian Universalist Purposes and Principles state, "We covenant to affirm and promote . . . a free and responsible search for truth and meaning," conveying much the same idea—that truth is not really something we possess once and for all but something for which we struggle over a lifetime.

This understanding of truth is somewhat more nebulous than the creeds and catechisms, duties and dogmas from which many of us have departed. While the comfort of absolute confidence in what is true is appealing, Unitarian Universalists choose the discomfort of needing to experience that truth in their own lives. In the choice between truth and repose, we choose the former.

Mark Twain once said, "When in doubt tell the truth. It will confound your enemies and astound your friends." He continued that he had never known a real truth seeker. Sooner or later, he said, everyone engaged in the search for truth found what they were looking for and gave up the quest.

Protestant theologian Paul Tillich puts it somewhat more eloquently: "The castle of undoubted certitude is not built on the rock of reality." And later he sermonized on Pilate's question to Jesus in the Gospels, "What Is Truth?" "The passion for truth is silenced by answers which have the weight of undisputed authority. . . . Don't give in too quickly to those who want to alleviate your anxiety about truth. Don't be seduced into a truth which is not really your truth, even if the seducer is your church or your party, or your parental tradition." A "passion for truth" sums up one of the core convictions of Unitarian Universalism. Our doubt that we have found absolute truth already is not based on a lack of concern with truth. Our passion is learning the truth of the world in which we live and our way of living in it, in the words of Emerson, "converting life into truth."

But what is truth, and how do we know if we have found it? Psychoanalyst Carl Jung says there are really two kinds of truth—objective and subjective. Objective truth is that which can be proved, as scientists can prove that the Earth travels about the sun, that two molecules of hydrogen and one of oxygen inevitably constitute water in one of its forms, that what goes up must come down. This is truth that is universally accepted and verifiable. Subjective truth, however, is another matter. This is the religious truth that guides and directs our lives. What is true for me is perhaps not true for you. For born-again Christians, it is subjectively true that Jesus Christ is Lord and Savior. That is a central truth of their lives that cannot be refuted. Likewise a more Unitarian Universalist belief in Jesus as a man for others cannot be refuted. We can deny the miracles surrounding Jesus—the virgin birth, walking on water, the resurrection—by appeals to objective truth. Religious fundamentalists probably would not accept that, of course, but we can still make the case with confidence in the objective truth of what we claim. What we cannot deny is the impact of the idea of Jesus the Christ. Whether the lives of believers are transformed for good over time is yet to be demonstrated. Our lives will also have to demonstrate the power of our belief in the human prophet from Nazareth.

Pablo Picasso once said, "We all know that art is not truth. Art is a lie that makes us realize truth. At least the truth that is given us to understand." He discovered the elemental truth about human beings and events and portrayed it on canvas. In his depiction of the mass bombing of the Spanish village of Guernica, for example, he pointed to the truth that war is hell but hope rises out of the ashes; an arm with a lamp stands out in the midst of destruction. Einstein, on the other hand, found truth in his formula $E = MC^2$—energy equals mass times the speed of light squared. This equation points to the truth of physics inherent in the cosmos. "Truth," he said, "is what stands the test of experience." Presumably this formulation is still useful for scientists.

Who is to say whether subjective or objective truth is more valid? In religion, subjective truth might be the feeling that God comforts one who is in trouble. We can't prove this, but for the believer it is true. It is true in Picasso's sense of truth but not in Einstein's, for one cannot prove the existence of God by scientific means. Jesus Christ may not be Lord and Savior for Unitarian Universalists, but it may be a truth for a friend or neighbor. We can neither prove nor disprove that someone is "saved," but no one can prove that we are not.

Parker Palmer calls the search for religious truth "the eternal conversation about things that matter." That conversation is symbolized by the Chinese ideogram for truth, two people talking. In this intriguing understanding, truth is not something handed down from on high but something created in the constant dialogue thoughtful people have always had over matters of ultimate importance.

How desperately we need such a "conversation about things that matter" is illustrated by Kahlil Gibran's parable about four frogs. They are sitting peaceably on a log when it is caught by a current and carried into a swiftly flowing river. One frog credits the log with having life; a second says the river, walking to the sea, carried the log on its back; the third frog says that neither the log nor the river was moving but the movement was in the frog's thinking, for without thought nothing moves. The fourth frog says, "Each of you is right and none of you is wrong. The moving is in the log and the water, and in our thinking also." None of the first three frogs is willing to admit that his is not the whole truth and that the other two are partly right. So they get together and push the fourth frog into the river.

The fourth frog in this story is probably a Unitarian Universalist who believes that the discovery of truth is not a solitary affair but the work of community. The fourth frog understands the importance of conversations that matter, of dialogue on questions of ultimate concern. Each of the frogs has a valuable insight; no one of them has the whole truth. Each of us is responsible for finding truth, for contributing our small truths to the larger truth. We share the truth openly and honestly as we experience it in our living. I learn from you and you learn from me. None of us has a monopoly.

In this community of conversation and dialogue no one is pushed into the river by those ultra-confident about their monopoly of the truth. From this kind of religious hope and humility it is possible to learn something.

TRUTH AND AUTHORITY MATRIX

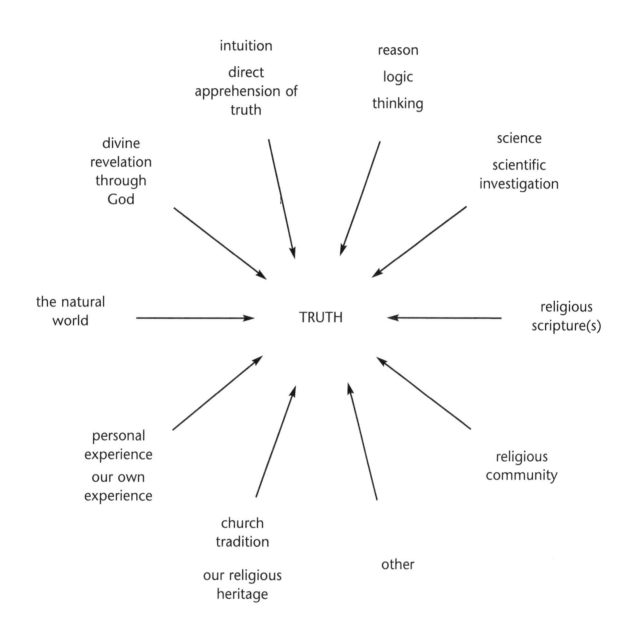

Truth and Authority:
What Do We Know for Sure?

Purpose

- To build group rapport
- To ascertain where the individual finds authority for religious truth claims
- To focus on our authority for truth, to test that authority, and to celebrate our common quest for truth

Materials

- Blank nametags
- Printed chalice symbols for each participant (available at www.uua.org/CONG/chalices)
- Scissors, pens, masking tape or pins
- Index cards or construction paper in different colors (enough to give seven cards or sheets to each participant)
- Notebook paper, pens, or pencils
- Copies of *Singing the Living Tradition*
- A copy of Genesis 22:1-19 and a copy of "The Blind Men and the Elephant" from *From Long Ago and Many Lands* by Sophia Lyon Fahs
- Books, journals, and articles from the Resources for reference and loan

Preparation

- Each participant should have a copy of *Building Your Own Theology: Exploring*. It would be best if copies were obtained or distributed before the program begins so participants can do the reading for this session.
- Ask participants to bring their writings from *Building Your Own Theology*, volume 1, if they have experienced that program.
- Ask participants to read the Introduction to this book (page ix); complete Worksheet 1, Credo Survey (page xviii); read the Reading for Session 1 (page xxiv); and read Genesis 22: 1-19 in the Bible.
- Ask participants to access www.beliefnet.com and complete the "Belief-o-Matic" and the "What's Your Spiritual Type" surveys found there. Those who do not have access to the Internet may be able to access it through the church computer or their local library.
- Read the Preface and Introduction to this program and familiarize yourself with Session 1 before the group meets.
- Provide refreshments for the first meeting, but make arrangements for the participants to take turns signing up for this task for subsequent meetings.

SESSION PLAN

Chalice Lighting   5 minutes

Light the chalice and read one or more of the following:

> What do you know—for sure?
> —Carl Sandburg

> Truth—is as old as God.
> —Emily Dickinson

> Truth comes to earth in small installments.
> —Clinton Lee Scott

> Let us accept truth, even when it surprises us and alters our views.
> —George Sand

The truth comes from a walk around the lake.
—Wallace Stevens

I am not afraid of the pen, or the scaffold, or the sword. I will tell the truth wherever I please.

—Mother Jones

Ingathering   15 minutes

Invite participants to draw or cut out theological symbols for their nametags. They may create chalices of their own or copy them from the chalice designs provided. Ask participants to write in the center of the tag, "Hello, my name is . . . and I believe . . ." (stating one affirmation from their personal credo.)

Invite group members to each find a partner for an initial theological interview and discuss what they each liked most and least about their experiences with the first course of *Building Your Own Theology*, what they learned from it, and what their expectations are for this course. After five minutes, ask each person to present his or her partner to the group for one minute, giving a comment or two about their experiences and expectations.

Orientation, Ground Rules and Contract Building   5 minutes

Ask participants to read the Preface to themselves or summarize it for them. If participants have not already read the material for this session, summarize it at this point or ask a volunteer to do so.

Truth and Authority   40 minutes

Give each participant two more index cards and instruct them to write on an index card one religious truth they cherish and why they believe it to be true. Refer them to the Truth and Authority Matrix chart (page xxix) and ask them to think about their source of religious authority. On a second index card, have them write one religious truth from their past that they have rejected and why they have rejected it. Form the group into triads and invite them to discuss their responses. When groups have had sufficient time for discussion, ask each individual to reflect on the religious truth she or he cherishes, and try to develop reasons why it might not be true, i.e., "if you were debating yourself on this issue, what would you say?"

After sufficient time for reflection, reform the triads to discuss responses—or discuss in the total group.

Referring to question 1 of the Credo Survey, ask the participants where they would place themselves on the Truth and Authority Matrix. Invite them to discuss with each other their individual movements among the positions on the matrix. Tell them to focus more on the authority for truth than on the specific truths themselves.

Alternative: Functional Ultimacy   40 minutes

Form small groups. Read aloud Genesis 22: 1-19, in which God commands Abraham to slay his son Isaac as a test of Abraham's faithfulness, staying the execution at the last minute. Unitarian Universalist theologian William Jones suggests a provocative question: How did Abraham know whether the voice that spoke was the voice of the God of Life or of Moloch, the God of Death? Jones suggests a concept of "functional ultimacy" to explain an approach to truth. Although we are not ultimate in the cosmos, we are ultimate in making our own decisions. We must decide for ourselves what our religious authority will be. Ask the groups to discuss this concept.

Alternative: Partial Truth   40 minutes

Have participants form small groups to discuss the story, "The Blind Men and the Elephant," as related in *From Long Ago and Many Lands* by Sophia Lyon Fahs. Read or ask a volunteer to read this Buddhist tale of a king who brought six blind men together and asked them the nature of the elephant. Each grasped one part of the beast's anatomy and claimed that as the whole of its nature. This suggests that each of us has only a partial claim on ultimate truth. Together we can develop a better picture.

Alternative: A "Wimp" Religion   40 minutes

A Unitarian Universalist church school student once asked, "Why is Unitarianism Universalism such a 'wimp' religion?" This was perhaps an expression of envy at classmates of more traditional faith who were calmly confident about the truth of their faith. Without surety of catechism and creed and even conviction that we have truth to share, we seem to lack a robust faith.

Discuss:

• How do we combine robustness of faith with integrity of belief?

• Can we provide "peace of mind" without stagnation of spirit?

• "Spiritual well-being" without deadness of soul?

• How would you respond to this student?

Homework for Session 2

• Remind participants to rewrite their credos based on what they have learned in this session and read the Reading for Session 2 (page 6).

Closing Ceremony   10 minutes

Ask each participant to take five index cards and do the following:

• On the first card, write your favorite of the quotations from Worksheet 2, Truth Texts (page 4).

• Write "Amen" on the second card.

• Write "Echo" on the third card.

• Write "Silence" on the fourth card.

• Leave the fifth card blank.

Instruct the group to form a circle. Ask each person to write one short, pithy "truth text" of your own creation on the blank card. Collect all five cards from each participant, shuffle them, and redistribute them so that each person has five different cards. You might begin the celebration by saying the following.

One symbol of our open-ended approach to truth is the image of the loose-leaf Bible in which "revelation is not sealed." Let us create the beginnings of our own loose-leaf Bibles in our closing celebration. As we move around the circle, each of you will take your cue from the card that is on the top of your pile. Read whatever text appears. If the card says "Silence" pause in silence and look to the next person in the circle. If "Echo" appears, repeat what the person before you did. After each turn, put that card on the bottom of your pile.

Conclude the celebration with these words: "From the cowardice that shrinks from new truth, from the laziness that is content with half truths, from the arrogance that thinks it knows all truth, O God of Truth, deliver us."

Or tell this story from the Jewish *Chassid*:

Two disciples of an old rabbi were arguing about the true path to God. One said that the path was built on effort and energy. "You must give yourself totally and fully with all your effort to follow the way of the Law. To pray, to pay attention, to live rightly." The second disciple disagreed. "It is not effort at all. That is only based on ego. It is pure surrender. To follow the way to God, to awaken, is to let go of all things and live the teaching. 'Not my will but thine.'"

As they could not agree on who was right, they went to see the master. He listened as the first disciple praised the path of wholehearted effort. When the disciple asked, "Is this the true path?" the master said, "You're right." The second disciple was quite upset and responded by eloquently explicating the path of surrender and letting go. When he had finished, he said, "Is this not the true path?" and the master replied, "You're right." A third student said, "But master, they can't both be right," and the master smiled and said, "You're right, too!"

Close the session by singing "Spirit of Truth, of Life, of Power," hymn 403 in *Singing the Living Tradition.*

TRUTH TEXTS

Whatsoever things are true, whatsoever things are honest, whatsoever things are just, whatsoever things are pure, whatsoever things are lovely, whatsoever things are of good report; if there be any virtue, and if there be any praise, think on these things.

—Philippians 4:8

It is worse than folly . . . not to recognize the truth, for in it lies the tinder for tomorrow.

—Pearl Buck

Be ye lamps unto yourselves; be your own confidence; hold to the truth within yourselves as to the only lamp.

—Gautama Buddha

I tore myself away from the safe comfort of certainties through my love for truth; and truth rewarded me.

—Simone de Beauvoir

The surest way to lose truth is to pretend one already possesses it.

—Gordon Allport

New occasions teach new duties; time makes ancient good uncouth; we must upward still and onward, who would keep abreast of truth.

—James Russell Lowell

I died for Beauty—but was scarce
Adjusted in the Tomb
When One who died for Truth, was lain
In an adjoining Room.

—Emily Dickinson

Reformers who are always compromising have not yet grasped the idea that truth is the only safe ground to stand upon.

—Elizabeth Cady Stanton

The thing is to understand myself, to see what God really wishes me to do; the thing is to find a truth which is true for me, to find the idea for which I can live and die.

—Soren Kierkegaard

Truth is great and will prevail if left to herself. She is the proper and sufficient antagonist to error and has nothing to fear from the conflict of free argument and debate.

—Thomas Jefferson

The question mark is an inverted plow, breaking up the hard soil of old beliefs and preparing for the new growth.

—Saul Alinski

Don't give in too quickly to those who want to alleviate your anxiety about truth. Don't be seduced into a truth which is not really your own . . . even if the seducer is your church.

—Paul Tillich

In relativizing history, herstory undermines the authority of biblical revelation to be the exclusive channel of truth.

—Sheila Collins

History warns us . . . that it is the customary fate of new truths to begin as heresies and to end as superstitions.

—T. H. Huxley

READING FOR SESSION 2

Philosophy has been described as a blind man in a dark room looking for a black cat that isn't there. Theology has been described as a blind man in a dark room looking for a black cat that isn't there—but finding it!

What have we found? We Unitarian Universalists pride ourselves on our theological diversity. But when does diversity so dilute us that we cease to become a cohesive and coherent religious community? This issue is explored by the 2004 Unitarian Universalist Association Commission on Appraisal. What holds us together theologically—if anything?

Clearly, it is not unanimity of belief, adherence to a single creed or dogma. Some say that this church serves the best theological potluck supper in town—a veritable smorgasbord of spiritual delicacies. Where else can you find such a theological Noah's Ark? Sitting side by side in the pews are atheists and theists, agnostics and pantheists, pagans and Christians, humanists and deists, and feminists and rationalists, along with those who refuse to be labeled or simply create their own labels. Yet here we are, gathered under a single roof, in a single worship service. Why are we here?

Is there or is there not a theological core that holds this disparate and pluralistic movement together? There may not be any single theological statement that ties us into one movement, but the radical openness with which we approach the spiritual quest is a uniting element. We can learn from the richness of our diversity. This diversity has been expressed in innumerable classes of *Building Your Own Theology*, which is not intended to be a debating society in which theists try to convert humanists, or vice versa. It is an educational forum, a small group ministry in which we share our stories, appreciate those of others, grow in our own faith, and give thanks for the opportunity to do so.

In more traditional churches, theological quandary is individual. In many creedal communities there are people who say the creeds but do not believe or hold differing opinions of them. But in our tradition, the quandary is institutional—different opinions are the norm. We expect and encourage religious diversity; we are quite comfortably—well, not always comfortably—multi-theological. We walk together before the immensities, sharing our imperfect wisdom and our incomplete answers.

I know there are people in many congregations who love the ritual and rhythm of more traditional services; those who long for the so-called "smells and bells" of a highly-liturgical church but who cannot bring themselves to accept what is required of them there. Our service feeds their intellectual appetites, but they remain liturgically hungry. "There is not enough spirituality for me," they say. But when asked to define what they mean, they often lapse into puzzled silence.

But for others, the lighting and extinguishing of the chalice create a cognitive dissonance; it challenges their rational faculties. They don't come for hymn singing and they can hardly endure the preliminaries that precede the sermon. "There is a little too much spirituality, not enough rationality here," they say. When asked to define their uneasy feeling about spirituality, their response is often puzzled silence.

And, of course, into this mix walks an unsuspecting innocent, a trying-to-please-everyone leader of worship—if one dares use that term—the minister. And he or she wonders, "How can I meet the diverse needs of these people? How can I, how can we, hold ourselves together? What is a theological mission statement that will satisfy everyone?"

One argument is that our theological glue is history—a discernible theological and historical tradition without which we simply would not be. We can look back to early church fathers like Origen, a third-century theologian who argued for a kind of universal salvation for all souls, or to Arius, who proclaimed a primitive unitarian position in a fourth-century debate over the trinity. Both were condemned as heretics. Our heretical roots are deep in Christian church tradition.

Our flaming chalice reminds us of this tradition—it symbolizes the light of truth, the warmth of community, and the fire of commitment. Its shape suggests the communion cup of John Hus, a fifteenth-century Protestant reformer who wished to democratize the Catholic church by having laity and clergy drink from the common communion cup. For his heresy he was burned at the stake in 1415. Followers subsequently identified themselves with a flaming chalice sewn into their clothing to commemorate his martyrdom and democratic spirit. The chalice also represents the

Grecian lamp of wisdom, which celebrates Socrates, the man who dared to ask, and other poets and philosophers whose names are beyond telling. We cherish the wisdom of prophets down through the ages from every age and tradition.

The circular shape of the chalice symbol comes from the Universalist side of our heritage and reminds us that we are ultimately one faith inclusive of all creatures, great and small. Faith for the global village takes universalism not only as a theological mandate for religious inclusion of all seekers but also as an ethical mandate to defend the dignity and worth of all people. The circle symbol also represents Einstein's concept that, ultimately, space is curved—thus linking the cosmos and human beings.

When we light the chalice, we are not merely scratching a liturgical itch or adding a bit of warmth and light to our celebration; it is not just an aesthetic act. It symbolically illuminates our part in a rich and courageous tradition that goes back centuries, if not millennia. If we truly realize what we do when we come together—what forces we release, what traditions we join, what memories we share, we would, as Annie Dillard suggests, all have to wear our hard hats to church—so powerful are the resonances if we take our participation seriously.

Some will argue that it is not the specifics of our faith that bind us in one religious community but the give and take of our theology—the exchange of deeply felt convictions. The method is the message. And there is truth here; we do build our own theology in a fairly distinctive way. Yet in an age where theological discourse is couched in very definite and substantive tones, it seems hardly enough to say that Unitarian Universalist theology is about agreeing to disagree agreeably.

Conrad Wright, one of our great historians, suggests that what holds us together is not that we believe together but that we walk together. He suggests that what binds this group of congregations and their people is not a common belief but a covenant to walk together into the mysteries, fully respecting diversity, relishing the opportunity to learn from one another, and vigorously discussing the issues that confront us. Instead of saying, "We believe together," we say, "We covenant together," promising to walk together in spiritual matters. We have chosen to walk together, in the words of Maxwell Anderson, "in a world where the lights are dim and the very stars wander."

So it is that each Sunday we open the offertory section of our liturgy with the words, "As a member congregation of the Unitarian Universalist Association, we covenant together . . ." followed by one of our seven Principles or one of the six Sources, affirmations that have been created not by an ecclesiastical council of denominational elders but by a long process of conversation in each of our congregations—a lively experiment in democratic religious community.

What is our theological core? What binds us together? I think each of several suggestions hints at the source of our unity: The richness of our diversity and the lively conversation it creates among us, our rich tradition of freedom in faith that evolves as the human race evolves, and our sense of covenant—a mutual promise to walk together not in unanimity of belief but in unanimity of intention to live the religious life.

However, the answer to our query still eludes us. While each of these rational reasons explains something of why we create a liberal religious community, the answer lies in something much more mystical, subjective, elusive, and experiential than any of them.

What holds us together is a very curious sense of being on an adventure of the spirit without a known destination. The song "The Journey Is Our Home" speaks to this feeling: "We move in faith, making love our creed, as we follow—the journey is our home."

Many new Unitarian Universalists have said that when they entered one of our churches for the first time, they had a strange feeling of being at home at last.

I am inclined to say that it is this feeling that holds us together—not reason, spirituality, history, or diversity, though all these contribute, but the feeling that we are on a journey together. Our theology is the result of the tough and tender experiences of life. It is not something determined by the church councils of old, even if reinterpreted; it is not something bound between the covers of any book; it is not the result or argumentation. It grows out of the warp and woof of human experience—the collective experience of the human race to which we are heir, the collective experiences of our fellow religionists over the years, and our own experiences—the events that shape who we are; the questions that are paramount in our lives. What really holds us together is less ideological than narrative. It is our stories intermingled with the stories of others and the collective story of humanity.

During the 1994 UUA General Assembly, the Reverend Carl Scovel, minister emeritus of Kings Chapel Church in Boston, delivered the Berry Street lecture. Carl is a devout Unitarian Universalist Christian, and he spoke of what he called "The Great Surmise":

At the heart of creation lies a good intent, a purposeful goodness, from which we come, by which we live our fullest, and to which we shall at last return. . . . Our work on earth is to explore, enjoy, and share this goodness. "Too much of a good thing," said Mae West, "is wonderful." Sound doctrine.

The Reverend Deane Starr, Scovel's good friend of thirty years and an agnostic and iconoclast, responded to the lecture. He disputed this "good intent," saying he found conflict and a cosmic indifference to humanity at the heart of creation. Deane, the humanist, found his sense of ultimate community with nature, not God, although he did not much distinguish them. Then this rational humanist stunned the assembled audience by leading "In the Garden," a hymn seldom heard among us. It had been part of Starr's pietistic upbringing, the feeling for which remained with him: "I come to the garden alone when the dew is still on the roses. . . . and he walks with me and he talks with me." Deane led the astounded ministers in singing it—most of them knew it! It was a strange but powerful moment.

Then Starr transfixed the assemblage again with this revelation:

My third son, Paul Michael, died of AIDS on December 31, 1992. I was positive that never again could I experience joy; I would have been content simply to find some release from anguish. I wondered whether I could find that relief by a return to the religion of my youth. Perhaps I could find comfort, once again, in the arms of Jesus. So I attended a little fundamentalist church in Naples, Florida. It didn't work; I left the service as deeply in pain as when I entered it.

That evening, I took a sunset cruise out into the Gulf of Mexico. The sunset was unbeliev-

able! The entire sky, from horizon to horizon, was aglow with color: reds, purples, pinks, and golds. Then the colors faded and that indescribable deep, deep indigo of late twilight filled the sky. The boat turned around to head back to Naples. There on the eastern horizon was a full and glorious golden moon.

With the tears streaming down my face, I realized that even though my son's being had been scattered, he remained a part of this awesome beauty. We can never contain the beauty in which we live and move and have our beings, but whether we live or whether we die, we are contained within this beauty.

Carl Scovel, reflecting on the experience, writes, "That gave me a new angle on Unitarian Universalism. It's a community where Christians give the lectures and humanists lead the hymns."

This story illustrates why we are here. It points to our genius, being radically open to human experience and to each other. That is the way we create unity of spirit among diversity of belief. Where else can you find a devout Christian and a passionate humanist, whose very understanding of the nature of ultimate reality differs so sharply, sharing such a common depth of human experience? Our theological core is experiential, not ideological. It is the highest common denominator of the tough and tender experiences of life. It is the sense that we are the meaning makers. Our clear religious message is that we can create a religious community without doctrinal conformity. We build the road as we go. The journey is our home.

In the love of beauty and the spirit of truth, we unite for the celebration of life and the service of humanity. Amen. Shalom. So be it!

Unity in Diversity: What Holds Us Together?

Purpose

- To consider and celebrate the diversity of belief among Unitarian Universalists
- To confront the problems such diversity presents to a radically pluralistic faith
- To become more comfortable sharing our differences

Materials

- Copies of *Singing the Living Tradition*

Preparation

- Familiarize yourself with Session 2 before the group meets.

SESSION PLAN

Chalice Lighting   5 minutes

Light the chalice and read one or more of the following:

A properly prepared liberal church is crystal clear, with the individual qualities of all the odd ingredients preserved; the soft things soft, the tough things tough, the green things green and the yellow things yellow. From this kind of heterogeneity it is possible to learn something.

—Grace Martin

In most other churches, theological quandary is personal. It is not institutional. . . . With us, on the contrary, theological quandary is not personal, it is institutional.

—*The Free Church in a Changing World*

I think one of our most important tasks as Unitarian (Universalists) is to convince ourselves and others that there is nothing to fear in difference; that difference, in fact, is one of the healthiest and most invigorating of human characteristics without which life would become lifeless. Here lies the power of the liberal way: not in making the whole world Unitarian (Universalist), but in helping ourselves and others to see some of the possibilities inherent in viewpoints other than one's own; in encouraging the free exchange of ideas; in welcoming fresh approaches to the problems of life; in urging the fullest, most vigorous use of critical self-examination. . . . Where opinions clash, there freedom rings.

—Adlai Stevenson

A Language of Reverence   45 minutes

In 2003, UUA President Bill Sinkford stirred considerable controversy with his call for a vocabulary of reverence, urging a reconsideration of the place of God in our collective life. Sinkford writes,

There are, for me, at least two important threads woven into the fabric of this conversation. One is whether we can name the holy, can we speak of that which transcends our ego and which calls us to the making of justice? Can we speak about God? But there is a second thread. Can we engage with the Judeo-Christian tradition? Can we reflect on those stories, using them to help us grow our souls, just as we reflect on stories from every other faith tradition on the planet? Or, because they carry too much emotional baggage, must we avoid the challenge and the wisdom of the tradition out of which we grew? I believe that both of these threads of conversation need to be a part of our dialogue.

Discuss:

- How do you respond to Sinkford's call?

- Do you miss this "language of reverence" in our celebrations?

- How do we find a common language that stirs our minds and hearts without offending the theological and liturgical sensibilities of others?

Theological Pluralism   30 minutes

Worksheet 3, Theological Perspectives (page 11), lists perspectives that might characterize most, but certainly not all, Unitarian Universalists. Based on these brief descriptions, ask participants to choose the one closest to their own view or write a brief description of another theological perspective not included. A more complete articulation of some of these positions can be found in the Introduction. Write a brief statement of why you have chosen this particular point of view.

Discuss:

- Why did you choose one particular position? Intellectual reflection? Personal experience?

- Is there any one of these perspectives you think should not be included in the range of UU theological perspectives? Why or why not?

- Is it possible for these various theological positions to exist within a single religious movement? Within a single UU congregation? Why or why not?

- What are the strengths and weaknesses of such a radical pluralism for sustaining and growing a religious community?

Alternative: Dogmatism Index   30 minutes

A pluralistic community requires not merely toleration of other points of view but respect for and a willingness to learn from them.

Ask participants to complete Worksheet 4, The Dogmatism Index (page 12), and discuss:

- How prevalent is dogmatism in UU churches?

- How dogmatic are you?

Homework for Session 3

- Remind participants to rewrite their credos based on what they have learned in this session and read the Reading for Session 3 (page 13).

- Ask participants to find a "holy" object that has special meaning for them to bring to Session 3 and prepare a brief word about why it is important.

Closing Celebration   10 minutes

Invite members to read their individual theological choice statements from this session. Then read the following by Barbara Wells and extinguish the chalice:

O spinner, Weaver, of our lives, your loom is love.

May we who are gathered here be empowered by that love

To weave new patterns of Truth and Justice

into a web of life that is strong, beautiful, and everlasting.

Close the session by singing "From You I Receive," hymn 402 in *Singing the Living Tradition.*

THEOLOGICAL PERSPECTIVES

Liberal Christianity

Unitarian Universalist Christians believe that we are inheritors of a rich tradition based on the Jewish/Christian Bible and the life, teachings, and death of Jesus of Nazareth. This view grounds us in a powerful heritage that we are called both to live out and improve upon. It provides a meaningful common language that addresses the basic issues of human existence.

Theism

Theists believe in a power, both transcendent and immanent, which we call God. God is a reality in which we live and move and have our being and with which we have communication in prayer and meditation. The divine is a cosmic process with which we cooperate to advance the cause of humanity. Most UU theists identify most clearly with process theology.

Mysticism

In the tradition of Ralph Waldo Emerson, Unitarian Universalist mystics believe in religious experience that affords an experience of union with the All-both with cosmic powers and with universal humanity. Mysticism becomes an important avenue to truth, which reason alone cannot travel.

Earth/Nature-Centered Spirituality

Earth-centered UUs (most would call themselves pagans) believe liberal religion is grounded in the natural rhythms of earth. Too many modern people have cut themselves off from these natural powers and resources. We need to recognize and celebrate nature and draw from it lessons for living.

Religious Humanism

Religious humanists believe religion is based in fundamental human nature and that appeals to any kind of deity do not satisfy the religious impulse. We should not arrogate to ourselves a sense of knowledge of the divine, but should undertake, in community, to create meanings and values for this life on Earth.

Other

Please briefly define any other religious perspective that appeals to you.

WORKSHEET 4

THE DOGMATISM INDEX

Answer true or false.

_____1. I grew up in a strict family in which punishment was important feedback for unacceptable behavior.

_____2. I find people disturbingly indifferent to what happens to others.

_____3. I believe everyone is the architect of his/her own fate.

_____4. Conflict is probably a good sign of a healthy community.

_____5. I don't believe in delayed gratification.

_____6. I doubt I would be willing to sacrifice my life for others or a cause.

_____7. I don't believe there is only one true religious faith.

_____8. I believe it is possible to live a meaningful life without a great cause to serve.

_____9. After all the facts are in, there is only one right answer.

_____10.I don't believe that most people know what's good for them.

Give yourself 1 point for each of the following answers. In general, the higher your score, the more dogmatic you are.

1. true, 2. true, 3. false, 4. false, 5. false, 6. false, 7. false, 8. false, 9. true, 10. true

5-10 points: You are inflexible in your thinking patterns and probably get into disagreements with others often. This may well prevent you from being loved or even liked. Try to be more open to attitudes that are different from your own.

0-4 points: You have convictions about life, but they don't interfere with keeping a receptive frame of mind toward the opinions of others.

READING FOR SESSION 3

The seriousness of the Unitarian Universalist spiritual quest goes back to the seventeenth-century Minor Church of Poland. Its adherents stressed church discipline, by which they meant the frequent reminding of individuals of their duty as faithful people in a religious community.

Each member was subjected to a quarterly moral and spiritual examination, followed by exhortation and correction from ministers and laity alike. Each member was expected to make an accounting of his or her stewardship. Although this religious faith was very influential in Polish history, it never grew significantly because its moral and spiritual demands were too strict. Such a practice probably would not fare well in contemporary Unitarian Universalist congregations, but it is not a bad idea for each of us to undertake a periodic self-examination and to ask not "How are you?" but "How's your faith?"

Spiritual life is often compared to a journey, as in John Bunyan's Pilgrim's Progress. We are forever taking trips, we mobile Americans, and we usually take adequate provisions. We have travel club maps and advice. We have first aid supplies in our glove compartments, games to keep the kids happy, and National Public Radio. We have a full-size spare tire, jumper cables, an emergency kit, and of course, the computerized global positioning system. We've arranged for neighbors to feed the cat. We pronounce ourselves ready to go.

Spiritual hunger, according to some, is the almost exclusive province of baby-boomers, who have been labeled "a generation of seekers" by Wade Clark Roof. One critical observer thinks this vantage point is limited. Joe Wakalee-Lynch sarcastically writes that, in this view, "Anyone born between 1946 and 1962 who ever had a thought beyond the next meal is a seeker."

Ultimately we are all travelers, all seekers—regardless of generation and regardless of theology. Soul-searching is the work equally of those who believe the finite soul needs connection with the infinite and those who believe we live alone without God in a random universe. Spirituality exists for the doubting soul as well as for the believing soul. Faith and logic converge in our quest. Even at our rational best, we observe that the most powerful cosmic forces are invisible—wind, heat, cold, the turning of the seasons,

human affection, and devotion to a cause. We can observe their workings but not determine why they do what they do. A creative power not completely comprehensible to reason and science is at work in the world. Human? Divine? Both? Neither? Perhaps we cannot know.

But what are we seeking? We seek at least to avoid a sort of sleeping sickness of the soul—the loss of seriousness, enthusiasm, and zest for living. In the story "Knights and Dragons" by Elizabeth Spencer, one character experiences an awful day and believes that he is the "world's most useless citizen . . . an impractical cultural product, a detached hand reaching out, certainly changing nothing, not even touching anything." The scene concludes with these suggestive words: "He longed for his white kitchen table and his wife's warm brown eyes, under whose regard he had so often reassembled his soul."

Reassembling our souls. Now that presupposes we have a soul—a debatable proposition at best—especially in a theological company of theists and atheists, deists and agnostics, humanists and pagans, scientists and free-thinkers. In Greek thought there is a bifurcation of body and soul, soul belonging to a divine, eternal realm, that undying, indestructible part of humanity that is confined to the body during life on Earth. An old Greek proverb reads, "The body is the prison-house of the soul." In Hebrew thought body and soul are indistinguishable. The word *nephesh* means "breath" and is often used to designate "a living being." In this tradition humanity is formed from the basic stuff of Earth. We are, in a literal and poetic sense, "clay that speaks." In Latin, *spirit* means "to breathe" or "to blow"; in the Christian scriptures it is *pneuma*, life force and vitality. The spiritual realm has to do with those invisible forces that create and sustain life, the very ground of our being. It is the inner dimension of things. The Buddhist doctrine of *anata* or "non-soul" denies the existence of a soul or any spiritual substance at all. Instead, human life is likened to a flame passed from candle to candle. Human life is ephemeral; our impermanence is like the grains of sand in a sand pile.

But these discussions of soul are too ephemeral, too poetic, too subjective. In our materialistic time, if we cannot measure something, it simply does not exist. *Soul* is simply one of those words that defies definition. Marcus Aurelius's colorful interpretations of body and soul suggest that the human race consists of "spirits dragging corpses around with them." Graham Dunstan Martin calls the soul the "ghost in the machine," or "the Angel in the Engine." Sir Cyril Burt writes about "perfectly healthy bodies staggering under the weight of dead minds" and "a carcass loosely coupled with a ghost."

Perhaps we might better think of the soul as poetry. We resort, or rise, to poetry whenever we're in too deep and cannot figure something out. Soul is poetry, best understood in flights of imagination or narrative. One of the most arresting portrayals of soul is in James Weldon Johnson's *God's Trombones: Seven Negro Sermons in Verse*. In "The Creation" he writes,

Up from the bed of the river God scooped up the clay; and by the bank of the river He kneeled him down; and there the great God Almighty who lit the sun and fixed it in the sky, who flung the stars to the most far corner of the night, who rounded the earth in the middle of his hand; this great God, like a mammy bending over her baby, kneeled down in the dust toiling over a lump of clay 'till he shaped it in his own image; then into it he blew the breath of life. And man became a living soul. Amen. Amen.

Both the scientific and the poetic descriptions of how we came to be are valid and both serve to inspire. Both have soul: The theory of evolution is majestic and Johnson's "Creation" is moving. One satisfies our reason; the other our imagination. We all know intuitively the truth in the words of Sophia Lyon Fahs: "We gather in reverence before all intangible things—that eyes see not, nor ears can detect—that hands can never touch, that space cannot hold, and time cannot measure.

Knowing all this, where do we go to reassemble our souls? Where do we go to catch our breath in a breathless time? Where do we go to weave together the strands of our lives? Where do we go to collect our scattered thoughts and fragmented feelings? Where do we find resting places for the spirit? Where do we go to center ourselves? We all need a touchstone, a place to reassemble our souls. We may do this reassembling with a loved and trusted one, in nature, or in solitary medita-

tion; it may be a special holy place like a monastery or in church. We all need some spiritual space in which to reorient ourselves to the life we wish to live, a sacred inner space that is inviolate.

Religious people must have a center; we cannot be all circumference. We need a transforming center from which we can move to the outer edges of our living. We need an orienting center from which to take our bearings in a world where, in Conrad Wright's words, the "lights are dim and the very stars wander." We need to explore our spiritual core in a world in which the old authoritarian gods are dead and we are in charge of our religious destiny.

How often have we heard someone say, "I'm spiritual, but I'm not religious"? A common distinction is made between the two. *Spirituality* generally refers to the private zone of human experience. *Religion* usually refers to the social zone. Spirituality is self-focused, while religion is community-centered. Spirituality, as stated by Philip Zaleski, may be thought of as the "inner lining of religion."

It is possible to develop spiritually both in isolation and in community, but much of contemporary spirituality deprives itself of an ongoing community of faith and is thereby impoverished. We have perhaps confused the container with the content. Religion can be seen as the outward form, the container, the worship service, the education program, the community outreach, the mutual ministry of the faithful.

Spirituality is that inner growth that happens in each of us, growth that is facilitated best when it is grounded in a community with a history, a world-serving mission, regular worship, and commitment to care for one another over the life span. Spirituality without religion can become amorphous, vague, and self-serving, just as water without a pitcher to give it shape spills uselessly on the floor.

To be sure, a deep spiritual hunger exists today. People want more meaning in their lives than they can find in the everyday world. But many seem to want spirituality on their own terms, without the rigorous ethical and spiritual disciplines of a community of faith like our Polish forbears. A church of one. No obligations save to themselves. Are today's spiritual pilgrims looking for the challenges of a deeper faith or are they merely searching for assurances that the way of life they are already living is pretty much okay?

This kind of spirituality is the flavor of religion without the substance. Spirituality is too often equated with personal success—whatever that means. However, life is about failure and success, victory and defeat, joy and sorrow, enjoyment and suffering. There is too much of the "feel good" mentality in what passes for the contemporary spiritual journey. Can it deal with the inevitable bumps in the road?

America is obsessed with spirituality; it is ubiquitous. Bookstore shelves groan with spiritually oriented self-help books. We are awash in McSpirituality: junk food for the soul, religion a la carte, or what the *Utne Reader* calls "smorgasbord spirituality." We already have a book entitled the *Index of Leading Spiritual Indicators*.

Poet Kathleen Norris worries about treating the soul "as just one more consumer on the American landscape and spirituality as the commodity that fulfills its every whim. . . ." At its worst, spirituality becomes just another consumable in the quest for a more fulfilled life, like a gym membership. Such pop spirituality "does not content itself with sharing the commonalties of the human religious impulse but seeks to elevate our ordinary narcissistic impulses into a religion." A friend told Norris of an address by a popular self-help author who defined "meditation as focusing on your plans for the day and thanking God for making them happen."

Consciousness guru Ken Wilbur critiques the superficiality of some New Age spirituality in these words:

We baby boomers have to be on guard against the belief that we're the only ones who ever got anything right. As if we're about to bring in 'a new paradigm'—whatever that means—that will heal the Earth and lead to the greatest transformation on the face of the planet. . . . That requires spiritual practice, not just mental thinking—and that takes many years to come to fruition. That's not a very popular message at a weekend seminar where people want to hear about how earthshakingly important they are.

We seem to reside in two different worlds—the outer world of the consumer culture and the inner world of the spirit. Dissatisfaction with the world of getting and spending seems to drive the passion for something more. Yet that something more often seems little more than a blessing of the seeker's status quo. Thomas More teaches us that we need a faith that helps us live "beneath the bottom line," the bottom line being one of American culture's transcendent symbols. We are inextricably enmeshed in bottom-line thinking. A poem by Fredrick Zydek closes with words that express our addiction to the conventional wisdom of this culture:

Once I had a dream. I stepped before the throne of God. He asked only one question: "Did you become what you were supposed to be?" "I'm not sure," I told him. "But when I died, I had so much stuff, it took three days to find me."

We have so much "stuff" that it distracts us from our pilgrimage. We might find the treasure right here among us in our religious community. For unlike forms of contemporary spirituality that glorify the private quest apart from connections with others, the Unitarian Universalist church provides a communal setting that ideally integrates an emphasis on personal search with a sharing and caring community. After all, one of our movement's basic principles is to "affirm and promote . . . acceptance of one another and encouragement to spiritual growth in our congregations."

The pilgrimage is complicated in our free religious movement, however. There are not many signposts along the way. But what should we take with us on our spiritual path? What are the intangible spiritual gifts without which we dare not make the journey? Shall we take the equivalent of the *Talmud* or the Internet? Here are some suggested provisions to consider:

A sense that life matters

Whether or not there is a cosmic eye observing our lives, it does make a difference what we are and what we do. Most ministers of religion speak of their "call" to ministry, some inner urging to give themselves to something beyond their own lives. It is a grave mistake to limit this sense of calling to professional clergy. Walter Brueggeman warns us that too many of us settle for "an uncalled life, one not referred to any purpose beyond one's self." Life does matter.

A sense of humor

Although life is serious business, we should bring along the ability to laugh, a way of gaining perspective on our finite selves in an infinite cosmic setting. Robert Frost writes, "Oh God, if you forgive my many little jokes on Thee, I'll forgive Thy great big one on me." As serious a man as Benjamin Jowett, master of Balliol College at Oxford University, writes, "We have sought truth, and sometimes perhaps found it. But have we had any fun?" If the trip isn't enjoyable, why go at all?

A sense of connectedness

We're only kidding ourselves if we think we can make it out here all alone. That sense of connection—to our fellow pilgrims, to the Earth, to the cosmos, to the Source of Life itself—is necessary for people of all theological persuasions. Poet Maxine Kumin describes herself as "an unreconstructed atheist who believes in the mystery of the creative process." The soul shrivels without connections.

A commitment to justice

Roy Phillips writes, "A sage once asked if there was more in his philosophy than meditation and quiet introspection. Was there a place for social action? 'Oh, yes,' he replied. 'That, too. Social action is another way of working on yourself.'" We cheat ourselves if we neglect the spiritual growth that comes through social action.

A conviction that the good life is necessarily messy

We must learn to live with ambiguity and love it just the same. *In Learning to Fall* Philip Simmons gives a moving account of living with Lou Gehrig's disease, a terminal and debilitating illness, and making a life of confronting it squarely. He concludes, "Some of us go willingly to the edge, some of us are driven to it, some of us find ourselves there by grace. But all of us get there at some time in our lives, when through the gateway of the present moment we glimpse something beyond. And when we do, may we open ourselves to wonder, may we surrender to the mystery that passes understanding, may we find ourselves at the threshold of this eternal life."

The actual world of imperfect beings, broken dreams, and illusory hopes is the only world we have. We must find whatever meaning we are able to pluck from life. The good life does not fall into neat patterns. Good and evil have no labels. We may not choose the perfect partner. Some problems cannot be solved. Not all stories have happy endings; most of them continue and end with a mixed blessing. Life is always unfinished business; it is radically uncertain. Muddling through is a virtue.

This is a spirituality for the doubting soul. Creation is not neat, no matter how scientists try to reduce it to its basic elements, no matter how philosophers seek to find reason in everything, no matter how theologians try to tie everything together in a divine package. It is full of caprice; surprise is around every corner—sometimes ecstatic, sometimes tragic. Creation wasn't really made for me or for anybody. It was just made. And we are fortunate enough to enjoy the beautiful messiness of it all.

The Nature of Spirituality: What Is Holy?

Purpose

- To explore the meaning of spirituality by reinterpreting it in liberal religious categories
- To share something of our sense of the spiritual with one another
- To celebrate that which is central to our religious faith

Materials

- Copies of *Singing the Living Tradition*

Preparation

- Familiarize yourself with Session 3 before the group meets.

SESSION PLAN

Chalice Lighting   5 minutes

Light the chalice and read one or both of the following:

> The word God has included two concepts: a Creative Power entering from outside, and a Creative Power that has always been inherent and within. Whether this question is answered in one way or another, the Mystery is not changed or taken away. Some word or group of words is needed to express the Creativity.
> —Sophia Lyon Fahs

> A large number [of students] are disaffected. They'll say, "Well, you know, I'm not religious.

I don't go to church or synagogue. But I'm very spiritual."
> —Alison Boden, Chaplain, University of Chicago

What Is Holy?   30 minutes

Ask the group to form triads to share with each other their "holy objects" and what makes these objects holy to their owners. After the sharing, ask them to display their objects on a table for the larger group and explain each briefly until the closing celebration. Some may want to browse among the objects and speculate on why they are holy to their owners.

Ask participants to write a few sentences in response to these questions:

- What does *spiritual* mean?

- What is holy to me?

Ask a few volunteers to share their responses with the group.

Finding the Holy   30 minutes

Ask the group to study and reflect on the quotations in Worksheet 5, Finding the Holy (page 20). Then, invite them to form groups of four or five to share and discuss their responses to the quotations. Instead of small group discussions, or in addition to the small groups, you may wish to have a total group discussion. Discuss how much diversity is present in the group and how much similarity is there in the responses to the quotations.

Alternative:
Spiritual Report Card   30 minutes

Ask the group to respond to the following:

- How are you feeling spiritually?

- Do you have a healthy sense of humor about yourself and the paradoxes of life? When in doubt, can you laugh at life?

- Can you deal with the inevitable tragedies of life, including death?

- Do you manifest your spirituality in the world so that people take inspiration from who and what you are?

- Does your faith overflow into service?

- Does your spirituality lift you and your life into larger frameworks of meaning so that you see your life as a worthy project, so that you take joy in the work of your hands and heart?

Alternative:
Hymn Writing   30 minutes

Ask participants to write one or more hymn verses to the tune of hymns 123 or 389 in *Singing the Living Tradition* on the topic "What is holy for me?" People may do this individually or with a partner or small group. Invite them to read the verses to the whole group and sing one or more as part of the session's closing celebration.

Alternative:
Signals of Transcendence   30 minutes

In *A Rumor of Angels* Peter Berger posits five "signals of transcendence." Beginning with anthropology, he holds that in human life there are empirical "signals" that are spiritual nourishment to us. These are "prototypical human gestures" found within the natural world but pointing beyond it.

Argument from order. Individuals and societies need to have a basic trust in reality and its essential dependability. When a child awakes from a bad dream, she needs her parent to assure her that everything is all right—the world and life; love is reliable. This is fundamental trust in being.

Argument from play. We are, among other things, playful creatures, in need of time and place to suspend the time structures of ordinary life. Berger tells of the fighting around the city of Vienna in 1945 during which, with the sounds of battle all around, the Vienna Philharmonic faithfully completed its scheduled concert. It was a gesture of play before the terror of death.

Argument from hope. This is the sometimes irrational hope for the future, an act of faith against all that would argue against hope. For instance, a very old person may plant trees whose fruits he or she will never eat.

Argument from damnation. There are times when our sense of what is humanly possible is outraged and something in us cries out for justice. Our word of judgment is absolute and certain in this case, as in the Holocaust, the massacre of My Lai in Vietnam, or the tragedy of September 11, 2001.

Argument from humor. Humor reveals the ultimate discrepancy between the world as it ought to be and the world as it is. The fundamental discrepancy is between ourselves and the cosmos in which we are fated to live. Don Quixote is a classic literary example of the value of humor, as its hero futilely but courageously tilts at windmills.

Ask the group to discuss:

- Do you agree with Berger?

- Can you illustrate one of more of these "signals" out of your own experience?

Alternative:
The Mars Trip   30 minutes

Ask the participants to form small groups of five or six. Have them read Worksheet 6, The Mars Trip (page 21), and ask them to try to come to a consensus within the group on a decision to the problem presented. Indicate that the conditions of the story cannot be changed. Ask each group to share its decision with the total group. Is there unanimity among the groups? Diversity? Is there a possibility of consensus among the total group on the decision(s) to be made?

Remember that you are trying to identify not only possible solutions but also the values implicit in the proposed solutions.

Homework for Session 4

- Ask participants to complete Worksheet 7, Values Survey (page 22).

- Remind participants to rewrite their credos based on what they have learned in this session and read the Reading for Session 4 (page 23).

Closing Ceremony   15 minutes

Ask participants to form a circle holding their holy objects. Invite each person around the circle to state briefly why the object is holy to her or him. Share this story by Wallace Bartholomew from the *Register Leader* and reflections upon it:

A few years ago an Episcopalian congregation sold their building to a Unitarian Universalist fellowship. The fellowship hung a curtain over an open space behind the altar in order to increase a feeling of intimacy in their meetings. At the same time, they found a need to put a new floor on the social hall, so they moved their coffee urn into the space in back of the curtain. A few days later, an Episcopalian work party returned to pick up some furniture and equipment which they had left. As the [people] were working, one looked behind the curtain. He immediately called his friends over and said, "Look here, it's true! They do worship a coffee pot!"

With our diverse theological backgrounds and proclivities, what, if anything, is "holy" to us? Martin Buber helps us here: "Nothing in the world is utterly foreign to the holy; anything can become its vessel. . . . There is no true human share of holiness without the hallowing of the everyday."

Close the session by singing "Now Let Us Sing," hymn 368 in *Singing the Living Tradition*, or verses written by members of the group.

FINDING THE HOLY

The "holy" thing in life is the participation in those processes that give body and form to universal justice.

—James Luther Adams

The articulation of a new perception of the ultimate . . . will arise out of the discovery and recovery of woman's experience...

—Carol Christ

When asked who he was, the Buddha said "I am awake."

—Harry Meserve

It is the creative potential itself in human beings that is the image of God.

—Mary Daly

The enigma of things deepens
Into the Fathomless beyond.
From mystery to mystery is the gateway
Into the streaming wonder of existence.

—Tao Te Ching

God is not a symbol of power over man but of man's own powers.

—Erich Fromm

Thank God, I'm an agnostic!

—bumper sticker

Perhaps God chose me to be an atheist.

—unknown

WORKSHEET 6

THE MARS TRIP

Our spaceship has crashed on Mars, and we're in severe trouble because it's going to take quite a length of time to repair the ship in order to return to Earth—perhaps as much as eleven or twelve months. We have a food supply, which, if carefully managed, will last a maximum of three or four months.

A particular metal is needed for repairing the ship. The metal needed is present on Mars but in very limited quantities. All of it that has been found by the Martians during many years of searching has been molded into a small statue representing the Martian God. The Martians have placed it on an altar in one of their temples of worship. There's no other place to get the metal without extensive mining, which might possibly take years. The Martians say their temple will be desecrated if the metal of the statue is used for our repairs and that their God will be angered and offended. The Martians are a small, dwarflike people, although fully human people. They would be unable to stop us from taking the metal if we should decide to do so.

—C. Dodder, *Decision Making*

WORKSHEET 7

VALUES SURVEY

Below is a list of twenty values. Your task is to arrange them in order of their importance to you as guiding principles in your life. Work slowly and think carefully. If you change your mind, feel free to change your answers until the final result accurately reflects your true feelings.

_____ character (inner integrity about values and how they are practiced)

_____ justice (fairness in the distribution of resources)

_____ joy (personal happiness in life)

_____ mindfulness (being fully aware of the world in which you live)

_____ salvation (some form of immortality)

_____ meaning (belief that your life has significance in the great scheme of things)

_____ equanimity (spiritual poise in the face of pain, suffering, and death)

_____ altruism (helping others)

_____ international order (relative peace in the world)

_____ beauty (living in a world that is aesthetically pleasing and stimulating)

_____ reason (belief that life and the world make intellectual sense)

_____ passion (ability to follow your bliss)

_____ spirituality (a holistic feeling of harmony with invisible powers)

_____ faithfulness (persistent loyalty to persons and causes beyond the self)

_____ intelligence (capacity to "connect the dots" of life)

_____ gentleness (a nonviolent attitude and practice that infuse your entire life)

_____ prosperity (possession of what you need to live the good life)

_____ self-determination (capacity to participate in decisions affecting your life)

_____ worthwhileness (a feeling that your life has mattered)

_____ love (a pervasive feeling of affection for all human beings, or _agape_)

READING FOR SESSION 4

The words *Unitarian Universalist* connected to sin and salvation are somewhat akin to oil and water. Since the great bulk of us came to our movement from some more orthodox group, it is not surprising that many have a visceral reaction to the mere use of these terms. Many join our movement at least partly to escape such theologically suspect notions.

But what do Unitarian Universalists have against salvation? Evidently, everything. We are a people who do not want to be saved, judging from how often UUs place that term dead last in Milton Rokeach's value survey. Saved from what? For what? We perhaps agree with George Bernard Shaw who observes, "Heaven for climate; Hell for company."

Nonetheless, are we in danger of throwing out the baby with the bathwater? In rejecting the creedal concepts of sin and salvation, we may also reject the valid core of experiential truths they contain. Are we rejecting intellectually what we may have to admit experientially?

Sin is fundamentally a religious concept, most often describing the relationship between God and humanity. Hence sin has come to mean variously rebellion against God, alienation from God, or simply falling short of our best selves.

Salvation most often means a kind of reconciliation between humanity and the divine. This theme has many variations: Salvation can be earned by humanity or given by God or some combination. It can be of this world or other-worldly; individual or social; instantaneous or gradual.

In the Jewish and Christian traditions sin began with Adam and Eve and their rebellion in the Garden of Eden. There is really no original sin in the Jewish tradition; rather the myth illustrates humanity's disobedience of God's will. In Judaism sin is breaking the Hebrew people's covenant with God. One gains salvation from sin in this world by good works toward the one sinned against, or in the case of sins against God, through sacrifice or prayer.

Christianity was a reaction against the idea of salvation by works in this world. Originally grounded in the high ethical tradition of the Old Testament prophets, salvation by works came to mean salvation by ritual, and it was this temple religion against which Jesus inveighed. Unfor-

tunately, the followers of Jesus, most notably Paul, distorted this attempt at ethical renewal and created a whole new system of sin and salvation. Salvation was to be attained by conversion in Jesus Christ, not by a process of reconciling oneself to God by good works. It became a salvation *from* the world instead of *in* the world. The prototype was not the ethical life pleasing in God's sight but the dramatic conversion experience of Paul on the road to Damascus. It was a matter not of humanity's action but of God's grace.

St. Augustine refined this doctrine in later centuries. He contended man's basic sin was pride— "a perverse desire of height." It did not mean merely a sense of exaggerated self-esteem "but the general inclination of all to overestimate their virtues, powers and achievements."

Most of us accept a conventional Unitarian Universalist view of human nature that holds we are essentially good and that our progress is "onward and upward forever." We tend to believe in "the power of men of good will and sacrificial spirit to overcome all evil and progressively establish the Kingdom of God," as the 1935 Universalist General Convention put it. This liberal spirit is captured in the late Leonard Mason's limerick:

> Come return to your place in the pews,
> And hear our heretical views:
> You were not born in sin,
> So lift up your chin,
> You have only your dogmas to lose.

Yet is it not one of our tasks as theologians to come to terms with sin, or human finitude, and salvation, our attempt to live with that finitude? How can we explain the creeping greed of American culture, the increasing incivility among us, the growing coarseness of our society, the prevalence of war in the world? How can we explain the "sins" of sexism, racism, homophobia, ageism, ableism, and a host of other examples of people who have missed the mark and missed it badly? How do we account for the perversity of individuals? And how do we respond to theologian Reinhold Niebuhr's words, "Actually the view that men are sinful is one of the best attested and empirically verified facts of human existence"?

Perhaps we will conclude with theologian Paul Tillich that human nature can best be described as "finite freedom." Human nature is finite; it has limitations of genetics, history, and culture. Within those limitations it is free—free to choose to exterminate six million Jews, free to face the gas chambers with a song on the lips, free to serve one's cause by suicide attacks, free to respond to evil with courage. Religious liberals, in placing so much emphasis on freedom, have tended to forget about finitude.

Somehow we must account for sin and salvation—Unitarian Universalist style. Sin is a fact of life. Sin is our capacity for excessive pride. It is no mystical quality passed from some mythical Adam to succeeding generations. It is simply an existential reality, a manifestation of our human finitude, an egocentrism that blocks human growth. Sin is a condition in which we think of ourselves more highly than we ought to think or have any right to think. It is the deception of equating ourselves with God, or if we reject that concept, equating ourselves with Promethean Man.

This sin of pride is pervasive. Ben Franklin writes in his essay on "Moral Perfection,"

In reality there is perhaps no one of our natural passions so hard to subdue as pride; disguise it, struggle with it, beat it down, stifle it, mortify it as much as one pleases, it is still alive and will every now and then peep out and show itself. You will see it perhaps often in this history. For even if I could conceive that I had completely overcome it, I should probably be proud of my humility.

As the first atomic bomb went off in the desert at Los Alamos, New Mexico, its creator, Dr. Robert Oppenheimer, could think only of a passage from the Bhagavad Gita: "I am become death, the shatterer of worlds." He has written that the aftermath of that experience left with him "a legacy of concern. In some sort of crude sense, which no vulgarity, no humor, no overstatement can quite extinguish, the physicists have known sin, and this is a knowledge which they cannot lose."

Contrary to what we who have put all our faith in reason, intellect, and education may think, knowledge is no guarantor of righteousness. Ovid says, "I see the right, and I approve it too, condemn the wrong, and yet the wrong pursue. For I do not do the good I want, but the evil I do not want is what I do." The apostle Paul said much the same thing. Or as Huck Finn says, "Being good is so much trouble, while bein' bad ain't no trouble at all." So it is with us.

If we wish psychological verification, we might turn to the late Abraham Maslow, who describes the "wonderful frontispiece" in an "awful textbook on abnormal psychology. The lower half was a picture of a line of babies, pink, sweet, delightful, innocent, lovable. Above that was a picture of a lot of passengers in a subway train, glum, gray, sullen, sour. The caption underneath was very simply: 'What happened?'" Indeed, what did happen? These innocent though self-aggrandizing babes became not-so-innocent adults who had failed to transcend their egocentrism. It's an old story, a result of the interplay of nature and nurture in as-yet-undetermined proportions. But the important point is that sin as stagnation is a human reality. It is a condition of the soul.

We are born in "original sin" then, not in some metaphysical sense or because theologians say we are, but because every individual is born with a powerful egocentrism. Sin abounds when we are unable to grow beyond that egocentric perspective. The wages of sin are death—not in the Pauline sense of eternal damnation but in the sense that sin is that egocentric self assurance that blocks human growth. Spiritually, then, we are as good as dead. Our greatest sin is in not admitting we are sinners, not admitting our human finitude, not admitting we need to transcend ourselves.

As we turn to consider salvation, however, it becomes clear that we are inextricably wrapped up in the paradox of our humanity, for the same dynamic in human nature produces both egoism and altruism. The same drives that emerge out of our perception of the world as our oyster and ourselves as its pearl also give rise to altruism, to a sense of service.

Take the helping professions as an example. While they are praised as the most altruistic of callings, they can satisfy the ego in a number of very powerful ways. The same drive that moves us to altruism can also lead us onto the tempting paths of self-regard and self-glorification. The secret of salvation is growing in some kind of healthy balance so that we are aware of our finitude and at the same time aware of our capacity for self-transcendence.

Salvation, in fact, means wholeness or health, and health, we know, is not static but dynamic. It is a metabolic process, and illness is an interruption of that process. The body, as we know, is finite and cannot escape mortality. But we also know it tends toward health. The cut on the finger tends to heal; the body throws off respiratory illness normally; the individual fights for life and has amazing staying power. Similarly, salvation is a process of growth, which sin interrupts. We are not sinners or saints; rather we are characterized by states of being that may be good or evil at any given moment. The growth that is salvation can be seen in three stages:

- Admitting that one is a sinner—that is, prone to actions that block growth. In this stage one recognizes that preoccupation with the self prevents one from expanding beyond the self.

- Seeking to expand one's understanding of the world beyond the egocentric view.

- Living so as to optimize one's own growth and contribute to the growth of others.

Most of us fulfill what Abraham Maslow calls "deficiency needs," such as the needs for security, status, and love, without which we simply cannot survive physically or psychically. These needs are on a hierarchical scale from basic survival needs on up. At the upper end of the scale "deficiency needs" become what he calls "being needs," the need to grow, to transcend the self, to serve causes beyond the self, to discover some meaning in one's life, to have "peak experiences" that transcend the ordinary events of everyday life.

Salvation, then, is not a point of arrival in either this world or the next. It is a process of growth energetically undertaken. Sin is yielding to our all-too-human tendency to see the world solely from the perspective of the self and to see that self at its center. To grow is to expand one's world beyond the self, or put another way, to extend the self to one's fellows, to the cosmos that is our home. Salvation is not a destination but a journey in which, as an unknown poet puts it, "great truths are dearly bought and dearly won."

Salvation for religious liberals is a kind of contract with ourselves that we will seek to be more tomorrow than we are today. No church, no creed, and no person holds the key. The contract is with ourselves: with the sometimes pitiful, sometimes powerful people who live inside our skins.

The highest mountain in the world is Mount Everest. For a good many years people have tried to climb to its crest. A growing number have succeeded. But the significant fact about Everest is not the fact that people finally reached its summit. It is the heroic and magnificent feat that for decades climbers have tried to reach that summit, and in the trying, as a score of books have testified, they developed the strength and insights of giants. The actual success, the business of standing for a few frozen moments on top of a pile of rock, had little more than a symbolic significance. The great meaning of Everest was in the trying, in the attempt. Salvation doesn't mean we have reached the summit or realized all of our visions. It does matter—very much—that we try.

SIN AND SALVATION WHEELS

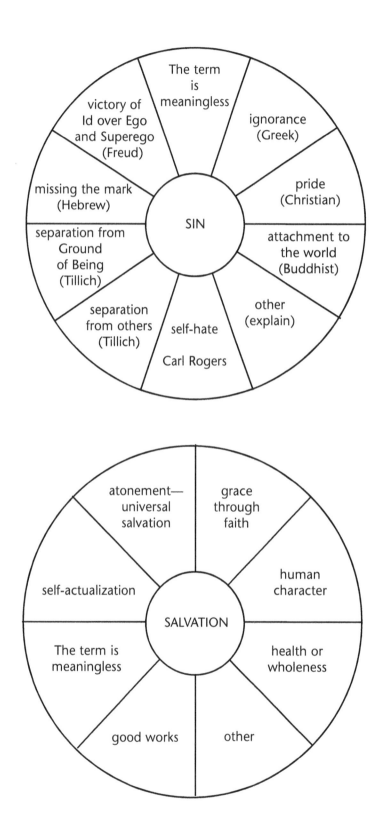

Sin and Salvation: Are We Saved?

Purpose

- To learn the varied meanings of sin and salvation and something of the history of these concepts
- To translate these terms into modern language
- To determine if these terms have a place in a liberal religious theology

Materials

- Newsprint, felt pens, masking tape
- Copies of *Singing the Living Tradition*

Preparation

- Familiarize yourself with Session 4 before the group meets.
- Tape two large sheets of newsprint on the wall. Label one The Seven Deadly Sins and the other The Seven Virtues. Number 1–7 down the middle of each sheet.

SESSION PLAN

Chalice Lighting   5 minutes

Light the chalice and read one or more of the following:

> The real sin against life is to abuse and destroy beauty, even one's own—even more, one's own, for that had been put in our care and we are responsible for its well-being.
>
> —Katherine Anne Porter

> Salvation lies in an energetic march onward towards a brighter and clearer future.
>
> —Emma Goldman

> There are no substitutes for words like "sin" and "grace." But there is a way of rediscovering their meaning. . . . sin does not mean an immoral act . . . should never be used in the plural. . . . sin is separation. To be in a state of sin is to be in the state of separation. And separation is threefold: there is separation among individual lives, separation of a man from himself, and separation of all men from the Ground of Being. . . . When despair destroys all joy and courage. . . . at that moment a wave of light breaks into our darkness, and it is as though a voice were saying: "You are accepted. You are accepted, accepted by that which is greater than you, and the name of which you do not know". . . . Simply accept the fact that you are accepted.
>
> —Paul Tillich

Seven Virtues and Seven Deadly Sins   45 minutes

Refer the group to the two sheets of newsprint you have taped to the wall and ask them to name as many of the Seven Virtues and the Seven Deadly Sins as they can from the Christian tradition. Ask the group to write them on their own papers to the left of the numbers. To the right of the numbers, ask them to list the sins and virtues that seem most important to them today.

When everyone is ready, write on the newsprint the traditional virtues and sins the group has remembered (see list below).

The Seven Deadly Sins	*The Seven Virtues*
vainglory or pride	prudence
covetousness	temperance
lust	fortitude
envy	justice
gluttony	faith
anger	hope
sloth	love

Discuss the following:

• What sins and virtues would you eliminate for the twenty-first century?

• What sins and virtues would you add for the twenty-first century?

Sin and Salvation Wheel   30 minutes

Summarize some concepts of sin for the group as follows:

For the Greeks hubris (pride) was a central fault, though ignorance can be said to be sin as well; we are not what we ought to be. The Hebrew understanding of sin can be defined as missing the mark, falling short of what Yahweh expects. Christianity has interpreted sin as originating with Adam's "fall" in the Garden of Eden myth. Augustine developed the concept of sin as pride, a perverse desire of height, a general human inclination to overestimate one's virtues, powers, and achievements. The Buddhist idea of sin is selfish attachment to the things of the world. Freud spoke of the victory of the id (our animalistic instincts) over ego (our rational capacity) and superego (conscience). Paul Tillich reinterprets the Christian doctrine in terms of separation—separation from the Ground of Being (God) or perhaps separation from others. Carl Rogers critiques the traditional Christian view that sin emerges from inordinate self-love by saying the basic sin is self-hate. Unitarian Universalists typically shy away from the term sin.

Ask participants to look at the Sin and Salvation Wheels on page 26 and decide where their view of sin is on the Sin Wheel.

After each member has had an opportunity to place herself or himself on the wheel, ask the group to break into clusters of three to discuss the different concepts of sin.

When time is up, say something like:

Salvation is another word religious liberals often avoid. Despite the fact that Universalism emerged by advocating "universal salvation," the final harmony of all souls with God, we tend not to use this term often now. We have reacted against the idea that salvation comes by faith through the grace of God. We have stressed good works but not primarily as a means of salvation. At one time Unitarians affirmed salvation by character, but that term is not currently in vogue. More recently some have spoken of salvation in terms of self-actualization or health and wholeness. Still, salvation ranks dead last in the 1967 Rokeach Value Survey among Unitarian Universalists.

Ask participants to discuss salvation in the same groups of three.

Alternative: Whatever Happened to Sin?   30 minutes

Discuss the thesis of Karl Menninger, who reopened the debate on sin in his provocative book *Whatever Became of Sin?* He believes that the disappearance of sin from our vocabulary dilutes our sense of guilt, answerability, and responsibility and leaves our civilization in deep trouble. By sin he does not mean breaking rules of the church or state, but the willful, defiant harm people do to each other.

Menninger rejects the criticism that he has sold out to the "law and order" philosophy which, he says, is not concerned with morality but with legality and vengeance. He traces the disappearance of sin as a concept to the rise of the school of psychology that holds that antisocial behavior is symptomatic of a pathology for which the offender is not entirely to blame. Sin, instead of being defined as deliberate wrongdoing, is understood as a crime or illness. Menninger believes this behaviorism weakens our social morality and increases our sense of apathy, which he believes to be among the chief sins of the twentieth century.

Tell the following story and discuss the incident in connection with Menninger's thesis above.

The late George Marshall, a Unitarian Universalist minister, writes of a personal experience in Boston while he is out walking his dog. He notices three well-dressed young males brushing by him and crossing the street. They begin to approach a young woman with a shopping cart. Sensing danger, the woman accelerates her pace. The young men then turn their attention to a seventy-five-year-old woman. After Marshall's attention is distracted by the barking of his dog, he looks up to see the woman prostrate on the sidewalk and the three young men fleeing with her handbag. Blood is coming from her nose and from behind her ear. Her glasses are broken. She has been knocked out of her shoes by the violence of the attack.

Marshall helps the woman get back home and reports the incident. He identifies the young men at the police station. They have taken $5.75 from her handbag—all she had. A lawyer for one of the young men later approaches Marshall and asks for his cooperation in helping his client "to get off," since he is the unfortunate product of the Boston ghetto. Marshall refuses. He writes,

> For years I have heard people say that liberals are too optimistic, too forgiving, too honey-coated to be able to deal realistically with the problems of the modern world, and now, I, too, had turned the corner . . . let us not be too hasty in forgiving those who trespass against us, for theirs is the upper hand and the clenched fist. Otherwise, the meek shall never inherit the earth.
> —*Church of the Larger Fellowship News Bulletin*

Homework for Session 5

- Remind participants to rewrite their credos based on what they have learned in this session and read the Reading for Session 5 (page 30).

Closing Celebration   10 minutes

In one sentence write your view of sin as you understand it. In another sentence write your view of salvation in terms of how sin can be overcome. Share your sentences with the group and then read these words from Reinhold Niebuhr:

> Nothing that is worth doing can be accomplished within one lifetime; therefore we must pray for hope. Nothing that is true or beautiful or good makes complete sense in any immediate context of history; therefore we must pray for faith. Nothing that we do, how-

ever virtuous, can be accomplished alone; therefore we must pray for love.

Close the session by singing "O What a Piece of Work Are We," hymn 313 in *Singing the Living Tradition.*

Once upon a time, someone asked the Almighty, "Why did you put evil in the world?" The creator of heaven and earth, day and night, the constellations and humanity, answered, "to thicken the plot." Perhaps one of the understatements of eternity.

In the wake of September 11, 2001, and the ensuing "war on terrorism," our curiosity as to why evil exists in the world has become insatiable. Issues of good and evil, God and Satan, have been much debated in the religious world. Unitarian Universalists tend to reject this cosmic ruminating, this tendency to anthropomorphize God and efforts to guess at God's thinking. What went wrong? Why, with so marvelous a garden, have we managed to spoil so much fruit and to plant so many seeds that did not ripen? Why, when we are given so much, do we experience war and strife, hunger and hate? And what has happened to the human spirit?

A funny thing happened on the way to the Kingdom of God, the Beloved Community, Utopia, or whatever one may call it. Ogden Nash sums it up well, "Progress may have been all right once, but it went on too long." The escalator of progress seems to have gotten stuck in the twenty-first century. In the twentieth century two world wars, economic upheaval, Vietnam, Watergate, and the beginnings of our current socioeconomic and spiritual malaise gave the lie to the idea of perpetual progress. The deterioration of the environment, the growing gap between the haves and the have-nots, and the threat of nuclear annihilation challenged us at the very roots of our faith. We are not without resources to think through this dilemma. Peoples of the past grappled with similar issues. It is time to learn from the past, and formulate a faith that will enable us to live in the paradox of human history and the human condition.

Eschatology is the study of final or ultimate matters, our own ultimate destiny and the fate of humanity, the struggle of good and evil and the survival of our world and being. Most of us are so immersed in the present that such issues (death excepted, perhaps) are not high in our consciousness. Nevertheless, our views of the future of the human race, planet Earth, and of creation are important to us as we seek to discern our personal roles in the great scheme of things. Religion tries to

give us a handle on them. It seeks to reduce these unfathomable depths into terms we can handle.

Eschatology flies in the face of our liberal religious tradition. After all, James Freeman Clark summarizes his liberal faith in 1885 by affirming "the progress of mankind onward and upward forever." Liberals in those days and after undergirded this optimism with the philosophy that harmony is the law of life—in nature, in economics, and in religion. Our roots are in the rationalist's tradition, which regards progress as the very purpose of creation. Unitarian Universalists have historically been an optimistic people, affirming the final triumph of good over evil, the final harmony of all souls with God.

Universalists meeting in Washington, DC, in 1935, adopted an Avowal of Faith—not a creed but a statement of principles. One article of that faith is belief "in the power of men of good will and sacrificial spirit to overcome all evil and progressively establish The Kingdom of God." Such confidence in the aftermath of a savage war and in the midst of a stultifying depression only attests to the incredibly optimistic faith that marks our movement.

This faith in goodness, in progress, this denial of the demonic and the tragic, amazingly overlooked the reality of human history. The faithful believed one could translate the natural order, which science was discovering in the eighteenth and nineteenth centuries, into social language. Social reality could be grasped and changed if people only had the will to do so. What was overlooked in applying evolution to the social order was that we cannot become so enamored of the loveliness of nature as to be blind to its terrible aspects. And did not Tennyson write of nature as "red in tooth and claw"? We never listened. We didn't learn that in the wake of political revolution often comes brutal repression—that pride in nation goeth before the arrogance of power; freedom that constructs a new Bastille suggests the ambiguous nature of human existence and human history.

We had forgotten that nature and history exhibit both creative and destructive powers, both a will to harmony and a will to power. History simply does not follow logical progression in an ever more civilized evolutionary spiral. The same perverse tendencies that led primitive peoples to pummel each other permeate our well-dressed diplomats as they calmly calculate nuclear annihilation. Humanity is both fated and free. It cannot escape its creatureliness. After all, we are animals in a long evolutionary stream with the same drives toward self-interest and survival possessed by all living things; we are free to mold our own futures, but always within the limits of our animal nature.

Unitarian Universalists have over the years entertained too optimistic a view of human nature. We rightly rebelled against the doctrine of original sin, from which people had to be saved through the church; we rightly protested Jonathan Edwards' apocalyptic talk of "sinners in the hands of an angry god"; we rightly countered with a God of love who would save all people; but our historic protest was carried perhaps too far with the romantic notions of Rousseau, who sees humans as noble savages corrupted only by an evil society. We overlooked the very natural tendencies toward self-interest in all of us. We forgot that, as it has been graphically put by Isak Dinesen, "What is man when you come to think upon him, but a minutely set, ingenious machine for turning, with infinite artfulness, the red wine of shiraz into urine?"

In short, we have ignored evil, the tragic dimension in history and human existence. We have failed to recognize that progress has not stifled the demonic but given it new form. Atomic power may save or utterly destroy us. Technology brings us affluence and effluence. Symbolically Satan is the most persistent of all God's creations. We had two world wars and the Korean War and then Vietnam, a sobering reminder that the "best and the brightest" could be wrong; international economic disarray suggested that even with all our scientific genius and technological know-how we still haven't figured out how to establish a just social order. The environmental revolution reminded us that we live on a finite planet and ignore its ecological imperatives at our peril. It seems that perhaps philosopher Thomas Hobbes is right that the nature of human life is "nasty, brutish and short."

Unitarian Universalist poet e. e. cummings writes,

> pity this poor monster, manunkind:
> We doctors know a hopeless case if—
> listen; there's a hell
> of a good universe next door; let's go

Liberal religion needs some theological posture in the face of this. While fundamentalists boldly proclaim the end of the world as a punishment for our sins of pride and progress, we are scoffingly silent; while the sophisticated orthodox speak of the end of human history and the beginning of the heavenly Kingdom, we are strangely silent. Most of us simply have never thought about such matters. Eschatology in a Unitarian Universalist Church? We might as well try to do away with coffee hour, the real eschaton. We often live in a state of individual and institutional denial.

Only yesterday it seemed our justified confidence in the scientifically guided human enterprise rendered supernatural religion theologically irrelevant. Now, even our liberal confidence in the success of the human adventure is in doubt. The old optimism is gone. We do not know what to make of a world in which the very powers we have celebrated are counterproductive at best and destructive at worst. This question is no mere luxury for intellectuals, like debating how many angels can dance on the head of a pin. How we view ourselves in the total picture of creation says much about our morale and our will to continue.

Henry Nelson Wieman says evil is that which obstructs Creativity. But evil seems to be a power in the biblical sense. For example, racism as an evil takes on a life of its own. It is structural, institutional, and spiritual. But why think about evil at all? Because it helps us face the seriousness of our problems. It is anthropocentric—that which threatens human fulfillment, destroys life, and keeps it from flourishing in us. It is a dehumanizing reality. It is a power not of our own making. We can't just reduce evil to that which prevents us from reaching our goal. Evil has structural and spiritual realities that have a life of their own. Whatever it is, combatting it requires soul work.

Human evil has done far more harm than natural catastrophe. In *The Brothers Karamazov*, Fyodor Dostoyevsky puts into the mouth of the atheistic Ivan the final, irrefutable, and unanswerable objection to a personal or theistic conception of God. Ivan offers example after example of the cruelty of humanity, implicating God in that cruelty if God has the power to control it. He then demonstrates that the only possible religious answer is that human suffering will be justified in the final divine harmony at the end of history, but he rejects this suggestion saying, "I renounce the higher harmony altogether. It's not worthy the tears of that one tortured child who beat itself on the breast with its little finger and prayed . . . with its unexpected tears to 'dear god.'" Since any God who would tolerate the suffering of even one child is either infinitely cruel or hopelessly indifferent, our ancestors posited another world in which these cruelties would be rectified, a "fantasy of another world in which He would ultimately do a better job. . . . The traditional God who opposes human freedom is dead . . . . human moral autonomy is incompatible with the traditional conception of a personal God."

The Yin-Yang symbol appeals to many Unitarian Universalists as a graphic illustration of the struggle between good and evil. Taoism and Confucianism, those ancient Chinese religions, hold reality to be a dynamic tension between polar opposites. The small white circle within the dark half of the larger circle suggests there may be good even in the midst of evil. For instance war brings out sacrificial courage. The small black circle within the white half of the larger circle indicates there may be evil lurking in the midst of good. Human achievement may be blighted by the sin of pride, as when we split the atom and developed a catastrophic weapon. Good and evil co-exist in the cosmos and in each of us. Good and evil are inherent in the nature of things.

Soviet dissident writer Aleksandr Solzhenitsyn writes,

Gradually it was disclosed to me that the line separating good and evil passes not through states, nor between classes, nor between political parties either—but right through every human heart—and through all human hearts. Since then I have come to understand the truth of all the religions of the world: they struggle with the evil inside a human being (inside every human being). It is impossible to expel evil from the world in its entirety, but it is possible to constrict it within each person.

The cosmos is more organism than machine. It is self-generating, not a static construction. It is a single process, a great living system with its own built-in laws. Reality is a great body in which we live, not a huge machine with which we tinker. There is a great difference between these two attitudes.

The contribution of the West to this line of thinking is that it understands human history as linear, not cyclical as it is thought of in so much of the East. We hold a prophetic view of human history in which human beings shape their own destiny. Our problem has been excessive confidence, a kind of cosmic triumphalism in which we exaggerate what we might accomplish and forget the constraints of the life system. We have believed that we can bring in the Christian kingdom of God, the Marxist kingdom of the Right, or secular Utopia.

Somehow we need to combine reverence for the cosmic processes of Taoism with the Western prophetic understanding of history. Good and evil struggle within an objective reality. We must come to terms with it. For here we are, exiles from the Garden of Eden, people who have learned that the fruit of knowledge is often sour, if not toxic.

We religious liberals need to understand the tragic nature of history. That is, the very creative impulses that lead to amazing advances in our civilization often lead to the greatest demonic powers ever unleashed. At the center of our being is a paradox; at the heart of the creation are contending forces. Our love of country can be the trigger for war. Our technological breakthroughs in weaponry bring ever-greater insecurity as we take the power of life and death into our human hands.

Adam and Eve were told, "Your eyes shall be opened and ye shall be as gods, knowing good and evil." The genius who wrote that mythology understood the radical nature of human freedom. The whole point of the narrative is to introduce humanity to the reality that we are on our own now. We are alone in creation, and no cosmic lifeguard is going to tell us what to do when times are tough.

Good will come from cooperation with the creative process; evil is a kind of feedback when the universal laws of nature or history are violated. When we resort to violence, destruction inevitably ensues. When we exploit the earth for selfish gain, we live in a desolate land. Historically or ecologically there are no free lunches. All learning is accompanied by pain.

It is admittedly difficult to really internalize the radically open-ended nature of creation. There are no cosmic guarantees. We may not survive in the end. No one, no thing knows or controls all or even a very large part of what is going on.

History is an unending process of trial and error. Humanity is a great cosmic experiment.

It would be nice if we could choose whether we wanted the mindless security of the Garden of Eden with its lush flora, fauna, and boredom or to bid farewell to Eden, dare our freedom, and risk uncertainty. Happily or not, the question is frivolous and we are fated to be free.

The Yin-Yang symbol is helpful in understanding the basic ambiguity of existence—the side-by-side presence of life and death, joy and pain, good and evil, and the interpenetration of each of them. And so our understanding of history is not some linear progress in which some human or divine purpose is ultimately realized but a vast dynamic of forces in tension. Our task is to serve, as best we can, those life-giving forces, the sustaining, transforming reality by whatever name we give it, and by implication to oppose those demonic forces that stifle the growth of good and creativity.

If we as citizens and as religious people do not raise these questions and get on with the humdrum work of democracy, it might be said that all the world's a stage and all the men and women merely drama critics. In a 1970 performance of Joseph Heller's play *We Bombed in New Haven*, actor Jason Robards, playing a bomber pilot disillusioned by the Vietnam War, asked rhetorically what could be done to stop the carnage. He was stunned one evening when members of the audience took his plea not rhetorically but seriously and gathered at the stage in the middle of the play. These audience members were not going to let the killing continue. Exasperated, Robards exploded. 'What do you want me to do?' he cried. 'I'm only an actor!'"

Precisely the point. We are actors, historical actors, agents of change. If history is to veer off its suicidal course, it will be because of actors who take time seriously, who link learning and action because they are inseparable. But in actual warfare no one returns safely to the dressing room. Walter Kerr, a critic at that performance, concludes, "Our silence was to indict us, our refusal to act in the theater was to become our refusal to act in life."

While our lives are very concrete and very specific, they are set in a cosmic context. We are creatures bound by time, limited by death, finite specks of being between the stars. We hurt and heal, confront and comfort, laugh and cry. But we go on; we must go on. There are slivers of hope, symbols of inspiration. For example, the United Nations building in New York City was built on the site of former slaughter houses.

During the Gulf War a woman gave her minister a most unusual vase, standing over a foot tall, with graceful, curving lines, and a very heavy base. She had purchased it at a rummage sale as a flower container. Later she had picked it up and read the inscription on its base: "105 millimeters, M 14, lot 12c B Company, 1944." It was an artillery shell casing beaten into the shape of a flower urn. "They shall beat their swords into plowshares and their spears into pruning hooks. Nation shall not lift up sword against nation; neither shall they learn war any more." While Unitarian Universalists do not take the bible literally, in this case it might be well to make an exception.

Eschatology:
How Do We Account for Evil?

Purpose

- To introduce the concept of eschatology
- To examine the historic "easy optimism" of Unitarian Universalists
- To incorporate some understanding of the paradox of existence into our personal theologies

Materials

- A copy of *Beginnings: Earth, Sky, Life, Death* by Sophia Lyon Fahs and Dorothy T. Spoerl
- Copies of *Singing the Living Tradition*

Preparation

- Familiarize yourself with Session 5 before the group meets.

SESSION PLAN

Chalice Lighting   5 minutes

Light the chalice and read one or more of the following:

> Men never do evil so completely and cheerfully as when they do it from religious conviction.
> —Blaise Pascal

> For as a picture is often more beautiful and worthy of commendation if some colors in themselves are included in it, than it would be if it were uniform and of a single color, so from an admixture of evil the universe is rendered more beautiful and worthy of commendation.
> —Peter Abelard

Evil is related to emptiness. It fills a void. Where good is not consciously active and diligent, evil enters . . . . Let us accept our responsibility with more grace than guilt. Thinking collectively, let our liberal religious community remember that we are part of the whole, and if the whole is wounded, we are wounded as well.
> —Elizabeth Ellis-Hagler

The Celebration of Life   35 minutes

Read aloud the following passage from *The Strangeness of This Business* by Unitarian Universalist minister Clark Wells:

> No one is against the celebration of life. And that is the theological trouble with this bromide. Charles Manson believed in the celebration of life. So did Hitler. Life per se is an ambiguous good. It's not whatcha got but whatcha do with whatcha got. Religion is more than a mindless jumping up and down about how super it is to be alive. I do not celebrate life when I pray at the graveside of a young mother or wait through with the despair of a family in a hospital emergency room. Celebration of life? How inaccurate, unfeeling, even blasphemous. You don't uncork champagne and shout hallelujah for life all the time. Sometimes you just try to endure it, in pain. Mature religion reminds us of an ethical dimension and a tragic dimension which the phrase 'celebration of life' does not contain. Commitment to a way of life and the capacity to endure what life does to us are surely as crucial as expressing our jollity at the ambiguous vitalities about us and within.

Discuss:

- What is your reaction to Wells's thesis?

- What does it have to say about Unitarian Universalist understandings of good and evil?

Good, Evil, And Eschatology   35 minutes

Ask participants to complete Worksheet 8, Good and Evil Questionnaire (page 37), and discuss it in small groups or in the larger group. You may wish to compare the group's responses to the Credo Survey questions, completed for Session 1 (page xvii), with the following responses to the UUA Goals Committee survey of 1967:

> There is a power that works in history through humanity, transforming evil into good.
> *Agree 41.1%*   *Disagree 58.8%*

> There has been progress in the history of human civilization.
> *Agree 95.2%*   *Disagree 4.8%*

> If you agree, check the three strongest supports for that belief:
> Growth of science and knowledge *88.5%*
> Increase in moral sensitivity *44.0%*
> Emergence of a world community *50.8%*
> Elimination of poverty and disease *37.2%*
> Increasing human rationality *39.1%*
> Increase of leisure time *14.2%*
> Other (please specify) *2.9%*

> Our potential for "good" can overcome our potential for "evil."
> *Agree 89.5%*   *Disagree 10.5%*

The percentages represent Unitarian Universa-lists in 110 societies who responded to the survey.

Alternative: Beginnings of Evil   35 minutes

Divide participants into three groups. Give each group a copy of the book *Beginnings: Earth, Sky, Life, Death* by Sophia Lyon Fahs and Dorothy Spoerl. Have one person from each group read or summarize one of the stories described below.

Each is a legend that sheds light on the human predicament. Invite the group to discuss the story and develop a group interpretation of the story's meaning for presentation to the total group for discussion.

Tree of Good and Evil. Genesis 2–3 tells the classic tale of the creation of Adam and Eve. God warns them they must not eat of the fruit of the Tree of Knowledge of Good and Evil. They disobey and eat the apple and their eyes are opened; they see good and evil. God is angry and expels them from the Garden to experience both good and evil in their lives.

Yang and Yin and the Dwarf P'an Ku. This story from ancient China is the narrative behind the Yin-Yang symbol, which unites action and passivity, sky and earth, birth and death, good and evil. According to the story, the Yin and the Yang are both good.

A Box Full of Troubles. This is the Greek tale of Prometheus and Epimetheus, who decided to mold new creatures from clay and water. Epimetheus worked without plan and gave gifts from a box to each of his creatures. Prometheus planned carefully and at last created a human being, but there were no gifts left in the box. Then Prometheus stole fire from the gods to give to humanity. As punishment Zeus sent down Pandora's box filled with worldly troubles. Although Pandora opened the box and all the troubles escaped into the world, so did hope.

Homework for Session 6

- Remind participants to rewrite their credos based on what they have learned in this session and read the Reading for Session 6 (page 39).

Closing Ceremony   15 minutes

Invite group members to share their rewriting of the Avowal of Faith. As a closing reading share the following rabbinic tale of Heaven and Hell.

A rabbi speaks with the Lord about Heaven and Hell. 'I will show you Hell,' says the Lord, and they go into a room which has a large pot of stew in the middle. The smell is delicious, but around the pot sit people who are famished and desperate. All are holding spoons with very long handles that reach into the pot, but because the handles of the spoons are longer than their arms, it is impossible to get the stew into their mouths. The suffering is terrible.

'Now I will show you Heaven,' says the Lord, and they go into an identical room. There is a similar pot of stew, and the people have identical spoons, but they are well nourished and happy, talking with each other.

At first the rabbi does not understand. 'It is simple,' says the Lord. 'You see, they have learned to feed each other."

Read the following:

Now, therefore, since the struggle deepens,
Since evil abides and good does not yet
    prosper,
Let us gather what strength we have, what con-
    fidence, and valor,
That our small victories may end in triumph,
And the world awaited by a world attained.

Close the session by singing "Turn Back," hymn 120 in *Singing the Living Tradition*.

GOOD AND EVIL QUESTIONNAIRE

- Define "good" as you understand it.

- Define "evil" as you understand it.

Respond again to the following questions from the Credo Survey.

- Do you agree or disagree with the following statement?

  "There is a power that works in history through humanity, transforming evil into good."

  Why?

- Do you agree or disagree with the following statement?

  "There has been progress in the history of human civilization."

  Why?

If you agree with the above statement, check the three strongest supports for that belief.

_____growth of science and knowledge
_____increase in human rationality
_____increase of leisure time
_____increase in moral sensitivity
_____emergence of a world community
_____elimination of poverty and disease
_____other

Explain.

- Do you agree or disagree with the following statement? Why?

  "Our potential for good can overcome our potential for evil."

- Do you believe there are cosmic guarantees for the ultimate survival of the human race? Why or why not?

In 1935 the Universalist Church of America adopted the following Avowal of Faith. Please rewrite it to articulate your own beliefs.

We avow our faith in God as eternal and all-conquering love;
In the spiritual leadership of Jesus;
In the supreme worth of every human personality;
In the authority of truth known or to be known;
And in the power of men of good will and sacrificial spirit to overcome all evil and progressively establish the Kingdom of God.

READING FOR SESSION 6

There is a story about the first officer to cross the Remagen Bridge in World War II. He was a Nebraskan named Karl Timmerman. A reporter called Timmerman's mother at the Goldenrod Café, where she worked. "You son Karl has just crossed the Remagen Bridge. Do you know what that means?" the reporter asked.

"I know what it means to me," Mrs. Timmerman replied. "Is he hurt?"

"No. He's not hurt. But listen to this. Karl Timmerman was the first officer of an invading army to cross the Rhine River since Napoleon."

"Napoleon I don't care about," the mother said. "How is my Karl?"

Against the backdrop of world events with their cataclysmic proportions we live out our own lives. In the context of historic happenings, we assert the meaning of our own being. In the face of famous people, we dare to believe we are important in the great scheme of things. After a while we may become benumbed by it all and withdraw into our private cocoons. We are once more becoming isolationist, afflicted with moral myopia and compassion fatigue. Like the title of a recent book we ask, "Who cares about apathy?"

Yet try as we might, we cannot quite sever the cord between our personal lives and the larger world. And we attempt to make some sense out of the confusions of our time, some way to figure out what it means for us. It is not easy, and so we leave it to the experts. Then we criticize them when they fail, as they so often do. We should, however, seek some understanding of the larger stage on which we play out our brief parts. We do it not only for our own sense of spiritual well-being, but also because from time to time we may act on what we have discovered.

Some years ago on the British science fiction series *Dr. Who*, the hero was asked, "Do you think your puny efforts can change the course of destiny?" He replied with a canny wink, "I just might tamper with it."

Who was he to think he could change the course of destiny? Who are we to think we can "repair the world," as Judaism expresses its moral mandate? Fewer and fewer people even ask the question. More and more people are retreating from the public realm. In a nation of legendary volunteerism, the pool of volunteers is drying up.

A cartoon printed in the *Washington Post* illustrates our predicament: One character says to another, "I'm tired of pretending to care about everything. I didn't create poverty or AIDS. Racism isn't my fault. Why should I worry about it? I refuse to go on pretending. . . . I don't care. I never did and I never will!" After the speaker leaves, the other character thinks to himself, "Militant apathy—the ultimate freedom."

Apathy is a kind of freedom *from* responsibility. Our rampant individualism drives us to claim this kind of freedom for ourselves. We acquire and hoard both resources and time. What used to be considered greed—one of the seven deadly sins—is now touted as what makes America tick. More and more of us ask "what's in it for me?" and spend more and more of our time as couch potatoes, computer fanatics, and health-club addicts. Unfortunately human beings wrapped up in themselves make mighty small packages.

Then, too, certain kinds of volunteerism challenge the way things are arranged in our culture. Many of us are not truly persuaded the world should be differently ordered. However, one cannot read Jonathan Kozol's *Amazing Grace*, for example, without experiencing rising anger at the way things are. For instance, the seventh richest and the poorest census tracts in the nation are but nine stops apart on an eighteen-minute subway ride between East 59th Street and Brook Avenue in New York City. But where are the demands for a complete overhaul of the American social system in which most of us are so relatively comfortable?

Of course entering new and unfamiliar terrain entails a degree of risk. We're not used to conditions of privation and danger. For the most part inhabitants of the Unitarian Universalist world are rather secure.

And we are discouraged from volunteering because we are not really sure it will do any good. The media assault us daily with massive social problems that overwhelm our capacity to cope with them emotionally or to do anything about them. We suffer from paralysis by analysis. Or in the cynical words of the playwright Bertoldt Brecht, "The man who laughs has not yet been told the terrible news."

However, some respond to what Harvard's Robert Coles names "the call of service." Why do they do it? Why do they volunteer to serve when they could be watching reality TV, *ER*, a police drama, or Monday night football? Coles' book *The Call of Service* offers several moving personality portraits: One is of a young black student, Dion Diamond, who takes leave from the University of Wisconsin to do civil rights work in Louisiana. He is jailed on grounds of "disturbing the peace" for attempting to integrate a restaurant. Coles visits him there and wonders out loud, "Dion, your ideals and values apart, I'm wondering why you keep at this, given the dangers and the obstacles." Coles is stopped in his tracks by the young man's three-word reply: "The satisfaction, man." Diamond goes on,

> I'm meeting some really fine people. I'm listening to them tell me a lot about their lives. . . . Isn't that enough—isn't that a good reason to feel satisfied? If you can spend some of your life doing work like this, then you're lucky! There may be a sheriff out there waiting for me with a gun, but if he gets me, I'll die thinking: Dion, you actually did something—you were a part of something much bigger than yourself, and you saw people beginning to change, right before your eyes, and that was a real achievement, and that's what I mean by satisfaction. . . . . I tell you, this is a real privilege; I am doing something useful with people who are the salt of the earth! Every day I thank my lucky stars—I thank God—for the good fortune to be here. . . . The way I see it, this is the most important educational experience I'll ever have.

We create a sense of meaning when we invest something of our life in that which will outlast it—serving a cause, befriending the friendless, standing on the side of justice. It is energizing to think that we have tampered with the world and, however slightly, made it a better place. Looking back, those who were active in the civil rights and peace movements carry with them a sense of having participated in something terribly important, which even now has at least the potential to give them moral energy.

Many who volunteer to help others or work for a cause talk about a deep sense of gratitude—a clearer appreciation for their own blessings, merited or not; thankfulness for the opportunity to serve, to make a difference in peoples' lives, to repair the world. And volunteering can make us aware of our own moral and spiritual growth, a rare education in a self-indulgent culture.

But retreat from the public realm is a pervasive phenomenon despite attempts to re-ignite the fires of American volunteerism. While honoring and encouraging volunteer service, our belief in "justice, equity and compassion in human relations" may be expressed as social service or as political advocacy to change systems and bring justice closer to reality. To illustrate one dimension of the potential difference, let's look at the late Mother Teresa—by all accounts the most famous volunteer in the world. Unitarian Universalists would not agree with her on many issues, her adamant opposition to abortion and family planning chief among them. She dealt compassionately with the poor, but refused to use her influence to attack the causes of their misery. Her life of service to "the least of these" is a strong challenge to our liberal "do-goodism" but does not suffice. When we see injustice, we may well feel a civic duty to annoy the unjust.

Margaret Sanger stands in contrast to Mother Teresa. She was a public health nurse who day after day visited poor women who were plunged into despair by unwanted pregnancies. "These were not merely 'unfortunate conditions among the poor' such as we read about," Sanger writes. "I knew the women personally. They were living, breathing human beings, with hopes, fears and aspirations like my own."

Sanger tells the story of Mrs. Sachs, a twenty-eight-year-old woman who suffers from septicemia as a result of a self-induced abortion. The woman's doctor warns her that one more pregnancy could be fatal. She begs the doctor to tell her what she can do to avoid the pregnancy. The doctor says, "Tell Jake to sleep on the roof." Mrs. Sachs begs Margaret Sanger, "Please tell me the secret, and I'll never breathe it to a soul." Sanger is haunted by the request but does nothing. Three months later Mrs. Sachs becomes pregnant, attempts an abortion, falls into a coma, and dies.

Sanger leaves the deathbed scene and walks the streets. That night she decides that she cannot go on like this, merely witnessing human suffering: "I was resolved to seek out the root of evil, to do something to change the destiny of mothers whose miseries were vast as the sky." The Planned Parenthood movement grew out of Sanger's compassion for one suffering soul.

The two basic questions we must ultimately

ask are these: What should we do and why should we do it? We should try to repair the world, because in so doing we repair ourselves as well. The word *volunteer* is from the root *voluntas*, or choice, and *velle*, or wish. We don't have to do it; we do it because we want to. We are Unitarian Universalists bent on changing the world. We do it because it is part of our ministry as people of liberal religious faith. We do it because we know that if we are not involved in the solution we are part of the problem.

We are called then to look outward by looking inward. Do we think our puny efforts can change the course of destiny? Like Dr. Who, we might at least tamper with it. We do well to remember a Jewish legend of the "*lamed-Vovnik-Tsaddikim*," the thirty-six righteous people by whose merit the world survives. In every generation there are these thirty-six secret tzaddikim, saints. Nobody knows who they are, but were it not for their lonely example, the world would crumble.

George Templeton, an observer of nineteenth-century Unitarians, puts it prophetically: "They are sensible, plausible, candid, subtle, and original in discussing any social evil or abuse. But somehow they don't get at it." Whether or not Unitarian Universalists in the twenty-first century "get at it" is a matter for debate, but it is true that the struggle for justice has been at the heart of liberal religion.

In his essay "Society and Solitude," Ralph Waldo Emerson speaks of the need to both cultivate one's own spirit and help build a better world: "We must keep our head in the one and our hands in the other. . . . These wonderful horses need to be driven by fine hands in order to keep them an effective team." Emerson points out the need for a delicate balance between spirituality and justice.

We tend to think of spiritual matters as private, belonging to that personal and untouchable zone of the soul whence comes our strength. Social justice, on the other hand, is public, what we do in the world. Some suggest the two are not only different but opposite. Social action is both a product of our faith and the expression of it and is therefore essential to our spiritual health. We can no more remain outside the public realm of peace- and justice-making than we could absent ourselves from Sunday worship. Promotion of "justice, equity and compassion in human relations" is as vital as "acceptance of one another

and encouragement to spiritual growth in our congregations." Neglect of either is unthinkable.

As spiritual beings we need to overcome our narcissism, our nonstop celebration of self. The consumer society is devoid of meaning. In a materialistic age happiness keeps receding. The self-indulgent life becomes a spiritual bore. Authentic spirituality means breaking away from our egocentricity.

The personal and social dimensions of life are not in competition but rather two halves of a whole; they create and nurture one another. Social responsibility has too much centrifugal force; it needs balance from the centripetal spin of inward spiritual experience to bring us back to the center from which wholeness comes. Solitude and community, spirituality and social justice, are not in competition. The further inward we explore, the more we touch what scholar Huston Smith calls the water table of our common humanity. The more the unseen moves us, the more we understand the hidden bonds of community. "Religion," it has been said, "begins in mysticism and ends in social action." To be is to be for others. To be is to be of use in the world.

Many of us experience "compassion fatigue," but we find our patience strengthened by the words of Douglas Smithall Freeman: "Most of the world's useful work is done by people who are pressed for time, or are tired or don't feel well."

While we arrive at our political positions through reason, they are also full of convictions and passions. The experiences are transforming because people feel deeply and are committed enough to put their lives on the line. It is spiritually exhilarating to realize that in one's own small efforts, one is part of a great living stream of reformers, a great cloud of witnesses who seek to create the Beloved Community on earth.

One such reformer was James Reeb, a Unitarian Universalist minister who was murdered in the hate-filled streets of Selma, Alabama, where he had gone to participate in Martin Luther King Jr.'s campaign for voting rights for African Americans. Unitarian Universalists were urged to gather for the memorial service, at which King was to speak. Many dropped everything and went to Selma. They marched nervously through a cordon of Alabama troopers armed with long truncheons that they pounded into their hands with intimidating force. Despite the fact the marchers were unarmed and at the physical mercy of the troopers, many felt like members of a liberating army as they approached the Brown's Chapel compound to be greeted by the cheers of black residents and their supporters.

The sanctuary was filled to overflowing with a great crush of bodies. King's eloquent eulogy and the singing of "We Shall Overcome" with a cantorial descant of the Jewish prayer for the dead were simply overwhelming. It was a mystical moment—calling to mind Theodore Parker's words that "the moral arc of the universe is long, but it bends toward justice." The gathered worshipers felt that they were participants in the very making of history. There was a feeling of oneness—every race and religion was represented—shirt-sleeved farmers with sweat on their faces were there with nuns in full habit and clergy in every imaginable liturgical garb.

In moments like this we learn once again that there is a reality greater than ourselves, a "creating, sustaining, transforming reality" of which we are a part. While it transcends us, we are part and parcel of it—co-creators with it, in a limited but vitally important way. This power speaks to us through people of prophetic fire who constitute a creative minority; it speaks to us in the lives of ordinary men and women and children; and from the depths of our own hearts when we pause long enough and thoughtfully enough to hear and heed.

As we negotiate the new millennium we will need to do some serious soul-searching and some serious world repairing—the two go hand-in-hand. We of the liberal religious faith are slowly but steadily being marginalized, overwhelmed by a confident fundamentalist political theology that threatens to utterly engulf us. However disparagingly we may speak of the religious right, it has tapped into something very deep, giving its followers a spiritual rootedness in a dogmatic faith and a sense of purpose grounded in an absolutist politics.

We who eschew dogma and reject absolutism will need to work harder than the denizens of the right, for our faith demands more of us. We need the power of conviction even in the face of our ultimate uncertainty about the nature of reality and right and wrong. While it is perhaps better to be vaguely right than absolutely wrong, the very nature of our faith requires deeper convictions.

The times are dire, but then people who live under the prophetic imperative are always worried. Comedienne Lily Tomlin recently said, "No matter how cynical I get, I can't keep up."

We need to be mindful of the prophet Jeremiah, who even as he warned of imminent doom and approaching foreign invasion, bought a piece of land as a sign and symbol of hope.

Consider these words by the late Nick Cardell, a Unitarian Universalist minister who campaigned to close the School of the Americas, a training facility for Latin American police and military personnel who have been implicated time and again in violation of human rights in their home countries. For his civil disobedience at Fort Benning, Georgia, Cardell was sentenced to six months in jail. Reflecting on his experience, he writes,

Sometimes I'm asked how or why I got involved in this cause. One easy answer is because what we do to each other is my business. These people—victims and victimizers—are my people. And there is also a very personal need. When I was a youngster I scratched my initials into the middle of the highest steel girder on a bridge leading into and out of New York City. No one knows it is there. But I do! In my adult life I have wanted to find life-affirming ways to write my initials on the tree of life. As poet Mary Oliver put it: "I don't want to end up simply having visited this world."

SESSION 6

Justice and the Beloved Community: What Is Our Place in the World?

Purpose

- To examine the ways we live out our values in the wider community
- To evaluate how responsible we are for social justice
- To determine the role of justice in our personal theologies

Materials

- Copies of *Singing the Living Tradition*
- Newsprint, markers, and tape
- A copy of *The Giving Tree* by Shel Silverstein, if available

Preparation

- Familiarize yourself with Session 6 before the group meets.

SESSION PLAN

Chalice Lighting   5 minutes

Light the chalice and read one or more of the following:

> We will achieve justice in Athens when those who are not injured are as indignant as those who are.
>
> —Solon

> The church exists by mission the way a fire exists by burning.
>
> —Emile Bruner

> The pitcher cries for water to carry and a person for work that is real.
>
> —Marge Piercy

> The moral test of spirituality is justice. . . . You must not be afraid of small acts of mercy, for in the absence of the giant steps you take modest steps; small acts of mercy keep us from losing our capacity to connect with suffering, and if we lose that capacity, we are spiritually finished. . . . Cynicism is a tourniquet for wounded idealism.
>
> —William Sloan Coffin

Twenty Things I Like to Do   40 minutes

Ask participants to make lists of twenty things they like to do. To the left of the appropriate item, ask them to put:

- S for those activities that primarily have to do with the self

- F for those activities that primarily are connected with the family

- O for those activities that primarily aid others on a one-to-one basis

- W for those activities that primarily benefit people whom you may not know

Discuss the following:

- How do you feel about the balance of your coding?

- Are you surprised at the results of the coding? Why?

- Have you changed the focus of your activities in recent years?

- How do you handle the dilemma posed by E. B. White ("between the desire to improve the world and a desire to enjoy the world") in the reading for this session?

- Did anything from this exercise surprise you? If so, what?

—Adapted from B. Simon, et al.,
Values Clarification

The Giving Tree   35 minutes

Altruism is touted as the desired way of life—to be is to be for others. But there are issues here, one of which is raised in Shel Silverstein's book *The Giving Tree*, a contemporary parable of the altruistic life. The story is about a little boy, a tree, and their relationship over a lifetime. The tree gives up everything for the boy—until at last there is nothing left of the tree but a stump for the little-boy-become-aged-man to sit upon. That is the end of the story but not of the controversy.

When this story was read without introduction to a group of *Building Your Own Theology* participants, reactions were mixed. One woman hated it. Here was the tree—female in the book—giving generously of herself to an ungrateful boy who kept on taking and taking. The frontispiece carried these congratulatory words: "Shel Silverstein has created a moving parable for readers of all ages that offers an affecting interpretation of the gift of giving and a serene acceptance of another's capacity to love in return." Another class member had read the book years ago, had loved it, but was now having second thoughts. The discussion revolved around altruism—the total sacrifice of the tree and the self-centered boy who simply took and took and took.

It is not difficult to relate this to ordinary life— we all know persons who seem totally selfless. We all know people who seem totally selfish. Since the tree in the story is female, and sacrificial giving has tended to be a woman's role, feminist theologians find *The Giving Tree* a powerful illustration of patriarchy.

Discuss the group's reactions to the story:

- At what point in our giving do we give away so much there is nothing left of us and consequently nothing more to give?

- How do you feel about *The Giving Tree*?

Alternative:
Genus What?   40 minutes

Some years ago, then Brandeis University president Abram L. Sachar spoke out against the "good people" of every community who were indifferent, slothful, oversensitive, cynical, and tired liberals abdicating their social responsibility. He categorized them as follows:

Genus Cynicum: cynics who despaired of changing the world.

Genus Tranquillo-Rectum: those with an overwhelming desire to seek peace of mind.

Genus Dejectum: idealists who soon are frustrated when they get personally involved in trying to reform society.

Genus Vituperosum: people who talk a lot about social injustice but do nothing while belittling those who are more active.

Sachar paid high tribute to those with real moral stamina in every community who hold the line, knowing the most honorable objective of any society is not ease but adequacy, not serenity but fulfillment.

Discuss:

- How do you react to Sachar's model? Do you find yourself in one or more of his types?

- How responsible are we for the world when our personal and family lives consume so much of our time and energy?

- How do we determine the limits of our responsibility?

Alternative: Responsibility Continuum   35 minutes

Write the following on newsprint and ask participants to complete this sentence:

"Someone ought to do it, but . . ."

Then draw the following continua and ask participants to discuss where they place themselves:

Why should I? _____Why not me?

Apathetic? _____or _____Involved?

Homework for Session 7

• Remind participants to rewrite their credos based on what they have learned in this session and read the Reading for Session 7 (page 46).

Closing Celebration   10 minutes

Read one or both of these closing thoughts:

Give me causes, O God, to theorize, argue, talk about. Let me think of problems far away. Let me go to luncheons, dinners for tired celebrities with long speeches, speeches about causes. Let me raise money, money to support big offices with large staffs, staffs to do a little good for someone, somewhere far away. Give me causes, O God, causes to forget the miseries that are too close to hide. But don't, O God, don't let me be involved with people. People are too near. People may enter my home, may cry before my eyes. People can be hungry, ragged, even dirty. They may ask me to give— to give without publicity. People may be rude. They may ask me to identify with them intimately, when all I want is not to be involved. I want to be interested, God, yes, interested. Causes help me to be interested and informed. People get me involved. So give me causes, O God, to theorize, argue, talk about. Let me think about problems far away.
    —Vilma Szantho Harrington

You say the little efforts that I make will do no good: they will never prevail to tip the hovering scale where justice hangs in the balance. I don't think I ever thought they would . . . but

I am prejudiced beyond debate in favor of my right to choose which side shall feel the stubborn ounces of my weight.
    —Bonaro Overstreet

Close the session by singing "Love Will Guide Us," hymn 131 in *Singing the Living Tradition.*

READING FOR SESSION 7

"Standing on the Promises of Christ My Savior" is a familiar hymn in the Black Church. One black preacher challenged his listeners to action by saying, "Most of you aren't standing on the promises; you're just sitting on the premises."

Promises and premises. We are promise-making, promise-keeping, sometimes promise-breaking creatures. The theological word is *covenant*—biblically understood as a binding agreement between God and people. God has selected a people for special responsibility; the people must honor their commitments to their God. When faith is broken there is all hell to pay.

The preacher who spoke of sitting on the premises may have been referring to mere occupation of a pew. *Premises* might also refer to value assumptions about the religious life—theology, if you will. Both meanings have value.

Are Unitarian Universalists keeping the promises or just sitting on the premises, geographical or theological? In the words of the Robert Frost poem, "I have promises to keep and miles to go before I sleep."

What are those promises?

With some justification, Unitarian Universalist congregations are sometimes likened to mercury, taking on an incredible variety of shapes depending on the shape of the container. Members may ride off in all directions at once. Leading a church as a lay or professional religious leader has been compared to herding cats. Nonetheless it would seem our task as Unitarian Universalists is to help erect a temple of the liberal spirit on some specific architectural plan. Below are possible elements:

The liberal church is a community of celebration.

We come together at an appointed time and place to sing, speak, listen, learn, question, and dedicate ourselves to what we call the "Beloved Community." Nothing is more important in the life of a church than the one hour (or more) spent in common celebration.

Once a newcomer came to one of our churches that had a rather austere sanctuary, which was quiet in mid-week emptiness. She found that hall of worship rather cold and barren. Happily, when she came the following Sunday, she found it unaccountably warm, welcoming, and lovely. On Sunday there were people, the space was meant for people. Their presence creates the experience of corporate worship.

Church attendance is not often stressed among us. A ministerial colleague once wrote a defense of absent members. Another observed, "You can tell Mr. and Mrs. John Q. Citizen that it is important to be decent and honest; you can't tell them it is wrong to go swimming on Sunday. They know it doesn't matter to God whether they swim or not; they don't stop swimming; they stop going to church."

Sunday attendance is one of the few barometers that may be used to evaluate the health of a congregation. Attendance at church is one of the critical yardsticks for self-evaluation, more important than even membership statistics. Regular church attendance is one of the promises of membership in a church; it is not so much a promise to a minister as to a congregation. Every absence weakens the community and diminishes the worship experience.

The liberal church is a caring community.

It is engaged in a mutual ministry in which we accept our human responsibility for our neighbors. Today I am strong and you are weak; I share something of my strength. Tomorrow I am weak and you are strong; I need your strength. None of us is totally self-sufficient; from time to time all of us need a supportive community that accepts us as we are and helps us become what we wish to be.

Most congregations maintain organizational efforts, like some form of caring community program, to meet the personal needs of people. But the atmosphere is also important, an atmosphere that is as real for an institution as personality is for an individual. Most, if not all, Unitarian Universalist congregations have miles to go before they sleep in fashioning such a mutual ministry—there remain lonely ones among us who are ignored, hidden hurts that are not ministered to, suffering that goes without comfort.

The emergence of the Small Group Ministry or Covenant Groups has been one response to this crucial need. Small Group Ministry is a network of small caring groups in which each member of the congregation can participate. It is a human network that embraces all who wish to be included so that each person will have friends with whom to share the most burdensome and the most liberating moments of the life process.

The liberal church is a learning community.

All its members are engaged in a cradle-to-grave process of religious education by which they grow their own meanings, values, and convictions. No one is all-wise. We need each other's insights; our values need the critique of others if we are to grow in religion, if we are not to stagnate spiritually.

One might envision a mini-university of religious studies with all ages seriously engaged in a learning process. The teachers will be not only professional staff but members of the congregation who have much to share of themselves, their knowledge and their skills. Envision a multiplicity of learning activities, not duplicating the secular agencies but addressing the ultimate questions like the meaning of life and death, the aging process, the ethical obligations of learning to live together, an understanding of our own faith and that of others, and the religious imperatives for social responsibility.

The liberal church is a community of moral discourse and social action.

Any religious group that does not confront the broken world in which it lives is guilty of cowardice and irresponsibility. Each action, individual and communal, should come out of deep conviction and emerge from a foundational understanding of our liberal religious faith. Moral discourse must become commitment in action.

The congregation as a whole is as responsible for this dimension of communal religious life as it is for the worship service, the religious education program, or pastoral care and mutual ministry. While the spiritual has an inreach dimension, it has an outreach dimension as well. Spiritual gratitude and health overflow into the wider community.

The liberal church is a community of commitment.

It is sustained by the generosity of its members and friends, in terms of both energy and financial resources. This is the depth dimension that enables the church to function in its programmatic mode. No institution can survive without a commitment that is both broad and deep.

Some confuse the spiritual and the material—believing they are opposite, if not contradictory. But the investment of time, treasure, and talent in the life of the religious community is in itself a spiritual discipline. It is what James Luther Adams calls the "tangibilication" of values—making what is discerned spiritually actual in the phenomenal world. It is giving institutional expression to our religious values.

There have been many articulations of the nature of this religious community. Unitarian Universalist minister Max Coots writes,

> We make no claim of being exclusive keepers of a special revelation, nor presume to have all the answers by which to provide a fire escape for those who fear hell, or an automatic passport to those in hopes of heaven. Where two or three of us are gathered together, I only know for certain that coffee will be served.

A UU colleague in ministry, Ralph Helverson, writes about the First Church in Cambridge, Massachusetts, which was organized in 1636 and has stood in its present location for well over a century, "There are many people who would resist equally vehemently any move to tear this church down or to take it seriously."

To keep our promises will not be easy. Walt Kelley puts these words in the mouth of his comic strip character Pogo, "We have met the enemy, and he is us." The external threats to liberal religion, to democracy, and to social justice are real. Yet the thing we have most to fear is not persecution—it is indifference. At many times in our history the strong arm of political and religious oppression was lifted against us. We had the will to endure and to prevail. Those were dangerous times, but not nearly as dangerous as these times, when commitment to religious community is too often optional, casual, indifferent.

Unitarian Universalists have not fully developed a sense of institutional commitment. A pattern of occasional participation is the norm for too many people. UUs have tended to select a sermon here, a program there, and service when needed.

As there are seasons in an individual's life, there are seasons of membership participation. People often enter with a burst of enthusiasm;

they bring their children and their participation is high. Children grow up and leave home, family patterns change, people who were once the lifeblood of the church move to the periphery of involvement, families break up, and other community interests all compete with the church for time, finances, and energy.

One must respect the right of Unitarian Universalists to determine their own patterns of participation. Yet it does bring into focus the meaning of membership. Is membership an occasional involvement, or is it a lifetime commitment? Does it cover only the time when needs are high, or must it be seen as covering a time when needs have changed and our task is to help meet the needs of others? At times of crisis, like the assassination of President John F. Kennedy or the terrorist tragedy of September 11, 2001, our sanctuaries have overflowed with people who otherwise seldom darkened their doors. Someone had to be there to keep those doors open and the lights on.

The liberal church is a church for all seasons.

It has been there in good times and in bad, in season and out, when it has been popular and when it has been unpopular, when people have participated and when they have withdrawn, and all times in between. The church abides, trying to keep the promise. But a church for all seasons requires a membership for all seasons.

For the liberal church there are no cosmic contracts. It is continually created and recreated hour-by-hour, day-by-day, week-by-week, year-by-year. It does not recreate itself automatically but by the power of will of a group of individuals.

Building that road takes commitment in community. It is not enough for a liberal church to be a miscellaneous collection of rugged individualists. As Emerson said, "No member of a crew is praised for the rugged individuality of his rowing." There must be a blending of singular selves into something called community. This commitment, this community cannot be compelled; it has to be willed into existence by hundreds of individual decisions. Individuals need to see themselves also as members.

We covenant together and make and keep promises to each other, costly commitments of time, energy, and money. The free church is not really free. We learn this annually during the church canvass, a kind of religious ritual by which people determine the nature of their commitment to the community. Energies follow investments.

If Unitarian Universalists are really serious about their commitments, they need to create and nurture human institutions. Theoretical commitments to health will not build hospitals, verbal support of public education will not build schools, abstract commitment to religious values will not build churches to provide space for helping people celebrate, care, learn, and act in religious community.

Unitarian Universalists have promises to keep to those brave men and women whose causes and commitments they are proud to celebrate; promises to keep to their buildings, inanimate structures of space and light, brick and stone, that house the animating forces of a religious people; promises to keep to children that they may know a living and growing religious experience; promises to keep to the wider community that there will be at least one prophetic voice that cries shame on injustice and beckons us all toward the Beloved Community; promises to keep to themselves that they will do their part in building a religious community that will nourish their spirits in the days to come.

Martin Buber sums up the peculiar qualities of religious community in this tale:

In a town not far from that in which Rabbi Nahum of Tchernobil lived, some of his disciples were once sitting at the table to eat, and as they were sitting, they spoke of the account which the soul has to give of itself in its deepest self-reflection. Then it came over them in their fear and humility that it seemed to them as if the life of them all was thrown away and squandered, and they said to each other that there would be no hope for them any more were it not that it comforted them and gave them confidence that they were allowed to join themselves to the great Zaddick, Rabbi Nahum. Then they all rose, driven by a common desire, and set forth on the way to Tchernobil. At the same time as this was happening, Rabbi Nahum was sitting in his house, giving account of his soul. Then it seemed also to him in his fear and humility as if his life were thrown away and squandered, and that all his confidence came from only this one thing, that these eager men had joined themselves to him. He went to the door and looked toward the dwelling place of the disciples; and when he had been standing there for a time, he saw them coming. "In this moment," added the Zaddick when he told of the event, "did the circle close."

Individualism and Community: What Is the Role of the Church?

Purpose

- To examine the liberal church covenant
- To create a covenant for our church
- To discover the place of the church in our personal credos

Materials

- Copies of *Singing the Living Tradition*
- Your church's covenant or mission/vision statement if available

Preparation

- Familiarize yourself with Session 7 before the group meets.

SESSION PLAN

Chalice Lighting   5 minutes

Light the chalice and read one or both of the following:

> We aspire to be a more truly catholic church, a church without walls, open to mystery, responsive to need, with honor, compassion and acceptance for all, a church with music and poetry from the richly varied arts, liturgies and literatures of humankind, full of wonder, worship, and healing, a church of the questing, hungering human spirit, in awe before the miracle of consciousness, the mystery within and the mystery beyond.
>
> —adapted from Jacob Trapp

> We do not think that we ought to be ashamed if in some respect our church improves.
>
> —Preface to the catechism of Polish Unitarians in the mid-seventeenth century

What Is a Church?   40 minutes

Ask participants to rank in order the "Elements of a Doctrine of the Church" in Worksheet 9 (page 52). Share the rankings in small groups or in the total group. Encourage discussion around the question "What is a church?"

Toward a Church Covenant   35 minutes

A *covenant* is a common agreement among people regarding their obligations to each other, to the wider community and/or to the transcendent. On the basis of the elements in the above activity, ask the group to write a covenant for your Unitarian Universalist congregation. Examples of such affirmations can be found in *Singing the Living Tradition*, 471-478. Share the covenants in triads.

Alternative: Advertisements   35 minutes

Ask participants to write one-minute radio or television spots that introduce your UU society to the community. Encourage them to distill their society's religious essence to a very few words. Share in groups of three.

Alternative:
Promise and Performance
of the Church   35 minutes

Read this selection from Gibson Winter aloud:

> The true meaning of the church has given way to the manipulations of the organization. In place of the sacraments, we have the committee meeting; in place of confession, the bazaar; in place of pilgrimage, the dull drive to hear the deadly speaker; in place of community, a collection of functions. This trivialization of religious life has made the middle class search for religious meaning even more desperate. One begins to wonder after a time whether the search itself isn't pointless, since every church activity seems to lead further into a maze of superficiality which is stultifying the middle class community.

Discuss Winter's statement with the group:

- Does this reflect your experience?

- Are there religious dimensions in your Unitarian Universalist society's community? What are they?

Homework for Session 8

- Cut out the Philosophical Statements About Suffering on Worksheet 10 (page 53) and paste them onto index cards.

- Remind participants to rewrite their credos based on what they have learned in this session and read the Reading for Session 8 (page 54).

Closing Celebration   10 minutes

Share the results of whichever activities you have chosen.

Read "Love is the spirit of this church," reading 473 in *Singing the Living Tradition*, or read the following as described by Alice Walker in *Sent by Earth: A Message from the Grandmother Spirit*:

> In the Babemba tribe of South Africa. When a person acts irresponsibly or unjustly, he is placed in the center of the village, alone and unfettered. All work ceases, and every man, woman, and child in the village gathers in a large circle around the accused individual. Then each person in the tribe speaks to the accused, one at a time, each recalling the good things the person in the center of the circle has done in his lifetime. Every incident, every experience that can be recalled with any detail and accuracy, is recounted. All his positive attributes, good deeds, strengths, and kindness are recited carefully and at length. This tribal ceremony often lasts for several days. At the end, the tribal circle is broken, a joyous celebration takes place, and the person is symbolically and literally welcomed back into the tribe.

Close the session by singing "Where Is Our Holy Church?" hymn 113 in *Singing the Living Tradition*.

ELEMENTS OF A DOCTRINE OF THE CHURCH

Rank the following in order of their importance to you as the nature and purpose of a church.

A church is. . .

_____ an awakener of faith. By *faith* we do not mean creedal beliefs or statements. We mean a lifespan process of growing our own meanings, values, and convictions for living in the world.

_____ a center of religious celebration. *Celebration* is the appropriation with awe and joy of the Life that sustains our people.

_____ a counseling and caring center, a place of mutual ministry where we share deeply our joys and sorrows and learn to love our neighbors.

_____ a place in which we can help satisfy the universal need for experiences of transcendence, providing vacations from the burden of finitude and the tyranny of time.

_____ a place where we know we belong and are valued, where people are joined by a common commitment and similar theology.

_____ a place of moral discourse and social action from which we reach out into the world to help make the Beloved Community.

_____ a place that enables us to be instruments of personal growth and social change, providing both the motivation and the opportunities to be change agents.

_____ a place of respite where we can find peace in a swirling world and focus our energies on things that matter.

—adapted from D. Ross Snyder, "Twelve Celebrations" and
Howard J. Clinebell, Jr. , "Mental Health Through the Religious Community"

PHILOSOPHICAL STATEMENTS ABOUT SUFFERING

God sends suffering to test us. If we are worthy, we endure our suffering and are assured eternal bliss.

God sends us suffering because we have been evil. God withholds suffering if we are good.

Suffering comes to us from an indifferent universe, a universe of cause and effect. We can do nothing but accept that reality.

Suffering can and ought to be greatly reduced in our kind of world. Our task is to so order the world that human suffering will be virtually eliminated.

Suffering is an inherent part of the human condition. How we deal with inevitable suffering is one of the ways we find the meaning in our lives.

READING FOR SESSION 8

Nobel laureate Isaac Bashevis Singer was once asked why there is suffering in the world. He answered, "This complaint is also made in the Book of Job; it is also answered there. And believe me, the complaint is a lot more interesting than the answer."

Humanity has developed its own litany in response to what author Peter DeVries calls life's "eternal severities" and the meaning of human suffering. How often have we heard others say, or found ourselves saying, these words?

> My God, I can't believe this is happening to me!
> I'm so totally unprepared.
> I'll never be the same.
> My life's a failure.
> Everywhere I look now, I only see reason for despair.
> I just plain feel sorry for myself, that's all.
> I feel trapped in this useless body.
> Helpless, utterly helpless...
> I want to scream and I can't.
> What did I do to deserve this?
> I'll never make it through another day.
> I don't want to hear about anybody else's problems.
> Everyone is a stranger. I feel totally alone.
> I keep expecting to wake up and be healed.
> Why me?

As we ask these all-too-human questions, we receive all-too-easy answers—spiritual clichés like "Make lemonade out of lemons," "That which doesn't kill us makes us stronger," "Time heals all wounds," and "It was God's will." These bromides from well-intentioned people can be spiritually impoverishing when life is a broken arc. So what do we make of the pain? What do we do with it?

First, we try to make sense of it. *Theodicy* is the technical theological term for trying to explain the ways of God to humanity. In the context of suffering, it is simply the age-old question "Why do bad things happen to good people?" One of the first explorations of that question is the biblical book of Job, a literary masterpiece.

Job is an upright and prosperous man who is buffeted with all manner of afflictions because of a wager between God and Satan. God is proud of Job, a faithful servant, but Satan bets that Job would become unfaithful if only he had to experience some of life's shadow times—sickness, poverty, and death. God calls Satan's bluff and torments his creature. Job responds as human beings have over the millennia. He is angry and explodes, "Why me? I've been good!"

Job finally confesses his finitude before the Almighty—"Though he slay me, yet will I trust him." But Job is not satisfied with his own abject resignation and continues to question why he suffers. His three companions are not able to comfort him or explain the reason. Then, in one of the great passages of the Bible, God speaks out of the whirlwind: "Where were you when I laid the foundations of the earth? Who fixed its measurements? Who laid its cornerstone when the morning stars sang together and all the sons of God shouted for joy?"

Thus rebuked Job can only say "Though he slay me, yet will I trust Him." Forrest Church calls the Job story the "first anti-self-help book." Suffering is inherent in life; we can but accept our fate and move on with courage. In Job, human beings are finite creatures living in a mysterious cosmos and cannot expect an easy justice. God is an impersonal, inscrutable cosmic force. Writers for the so-called Deuteronomic school could not let the matter rest there—their "do good and prosper" piety had been assaulted. They could not abide the idea that bad things happen to good people. And so, they added editorial touches to the original tale and Job's fortune was restored with divine interest. Now he has seven sons and three daughters and presumably lives happily ever after: "And Job died, an old man, and full of days."

So where can we find the courage to accept our fate? The Buddhist author Pema Chodron writes, "When I was first married, my husband said I was one of the bravest people he knew. When I asked him why, he said because I was a complete coward but went ahead and did things anyhow."

Buddhism responds to the human predicament of the broken arc by the first of its Four Noble Truths: Life is suffering. Pain is part and parcel of the human condition. There is no point trying to evade or avoid it. The Buddhist tradition offers the story of the "mustard seed medicine." A young mother carries a dead child to the Buddha and asks him to bring the child back to life. He requests that the woman go first into the village and gather mustard seeds from any home that has not known death. Of course she returns empty-handed, realizes that death is universal and that she must bury her child and move on with living.

Humanity has developed many explanations for human suffering. One popular view is that God sends suffering to test us, giving us no more than we can handle. If we are worthy, we endure our suffering and are assured eternal bliss.

Nancy Mairs, a Unitarian Universalist woman with multiple sclerosis, has written insightfully about this issue:

Some people will say, "God never gives us more than we can handle"—which I think is utter [expletive deleted]. Because if God's doing the giving, then God routinely gives us much more than we can possibly handle—MS is one such thing. But I couldn't believe in a God who would do such a thing anyway. I don't know how people can practice a religious faith if they think of God doing such things.

Another philosophy of suffering has a certain currency: God sends us suffering because we have been evil and God withholds suffering if we have been good. That canard should have been rejected long ago—the book of Job symbolizes its inadequacy. The lives of the martyrs and the deaths of the prophets should tell us how blasphemous a notion this is. From the crucifixion of Jesus to the assassinations of Gandhi and King, it is clear the righteous often suffer. From the oppressive pharaohs of ancient Egypt to the callously indifferent in our own time who profit from terrorism and war, it is clear the evil often prosper. We all know good people who suffer, and bad people who flourish.

Belden Lane proposes a third school of thought that perhaps brings us closer to the truth. He maintains that suffering comes to us from an indifferent universe, a universe of merciless cause and effect—where we meet "a God of fierce indifference." We can do nothing but recognize that we are part of the "fellowship of those who bear the mark of pain," as Albert Schweitzer so eloquently describes it.

While I agree in part with this attitude, it is just a bit too passive for me. Some suffering can be and ought to be eliminated. There ought not to be starvation in a world that can produce enough food for everyone. There ought not to be poverty in a land of plenty. Much suffering can be ended.

This leads to a fourth understanding of suffering, which resonates in Unitarian Universalist thinking. Suffering can and ought to be eliminated. Our task is to so order the world that human suffering will at least be minimized. We are a proactive people; we are social activists; we want to change the world.

Agreed, but some suffering is endemic in human life. No matter how much we strive to reduce it, it cannot be eliminated. We are finite creatures in an indifferent universe. When all is said and done, we die. Unitarian Universalists need to realize that however much we want to be in control of our destiny, in many ways we are helpless before the inexorable suffering that afflicts us; pain is the price we pay for living. Suffering is less a problem to be solved than a mystery to be lived.

Finally, suffering can be understood as an inherent part of the human condition and an essential source of life meaning. How we deal with inevitable suffering is one of the ways we find purpose in our lives.

Mairs writes,

We see disability as a social construction . . . . I do not consider suffering an aberration, or an outrage to be eliminated at any cost . . . . It strikes me as intrinsic to the human condition. I don't like it. I'm not asked to like it. I must simply endure in order to learn from it. Those who leap forward to offer me aid in ending it, though they may do so out of the greatest compassion, seek to deny me the fullness of experience I believe I am meant to have.

Victor Frankl, the Viennese psychiatrist who spent years in a Nazi death camp, suggests that if we have a "why" to live, we can bear any "how" or "what." He found that in struggling through his pain, he created life meaning for himself. How we respond to our suffering is the last of the human freedoms.

It is, of course, dangerous to romanticize suffering as a source of life meaning. Baseball owner Bill Veeck debunks that notion when he says cynically, "Suffering is overrated. It doesn't teach you anything." That is, of course, a possibility. We have known—or have ourselves been—persons who are embittered by the pain we experience. It can make us small; it can suck out the best in us; it can strip away the better angels of our nature. Intellectually we know we should not be bitter, that we should transmute our pain into courage, that we should learn from our suffering, that we should even teach out of our hurt. But that is hard business, and we all know it.

Unitarian Universalists are pragmatists and activists; we want to control the world in which we live. We are distinctly uncomfortable about suffering when there seems little we can do to reduce it or to end it. In the book *Pastoral Care in the Liberal Churches*, the late Carl Wennerstrom, a Unitarian Universalist minister, presents the following thesis:

> Religious liberals have been so preoccupied with the transformation of society they have neglected the transformation of individuals. Our tendency in the face of suffering is to organize to eliminate it, to reform society, and above all to act against the causes of suffering. In so doing we deal with issues, problems and causes, not with persons.

Wennerstrom explores the biblical scene in which Jesus is carrying the cross to Calvary:

> The first liberal is there helping Jesus, but when the cross was placed in the ground and Jesus was nailed upon it, the liberal was not there. Perhaps he was off trying to get a stay of execution or a reversal of the conviction or planning for the future support of Jesus' family or the burial arrangements or getting up a petition to Rome on the irresponsibility of Pilate. The point is that he was absent at the point of the crucifixion—the time of personal suffering.

We might come to these four conclusions about life as a broken arc:

Pain, discouragement, and death are part of the landscape of being human.

Some suffering belongs to the structure of things and is part of our fate, like death. We can do nothing about it. Some suffering is humanly caused and we can and ought to alleviate these self-inflicted hurts for ourselves and for others, but we must face up to the fact life is messy. Some problems can never be solved. Some hurts are never healed. There are no cosmic baby-sitters. That is the hard truth of being human. As William Murray tells us, a little boy one day asks the great preacher Harry Emerson Fosdick why God puts all the vitamins in spinach and not in ice cream. Dr. Fosdick replies that he does not know why but that life is just that way.

Each of us matters, and so do our hurts.

Therefore, as we sit together on what Nicholas Wolterstorff refers to as "humanity's mourning bench," we need to listen to those voices from our own center that enable us to muster the passion to endure. Poet Ann McCracken reminds us, "The broken heart still beats."

Suffering shared is suffering halved.

We can live with any pain if we live in a caring community. None of us can do it out there all alone. That spiritual truth is symbolized by the simple ritual of joys and sorrows. By lighting a candle and speaking to our own beloved community, we know we are not alone.

There is a horizon beyond our immediate experience, a greater context in which we live and move and have our being.

Understanding ourselves in the larger picture of cosmos, history, and community helps us gain perspective on our lives and helps us heal. In our best moments we find meaning in the wounds inflicted upon us.

Sometimes that perspective is gained through poetry. Unitarian Universalist poet Pesha Joyce Gertler, puts it this way in "The Healing Time":

> Finally on my way to yes I bump into all the
>   places where I said no to my life
> all the untended wounds—the red and pur-
>   ple scars
> those hieroglyphs of pain carved into my
>   skin, my bones,
> those coded messages that send me down
>   the wrong street again and again
> where I find them—the old wounds—the old
>   misdirections

and I lift them one by one close to my heart
and I say holy holy.

Sometimes that perspective comes to us through humor. An ad in a British newspaper describes a lost cat: "old, mangy, one-eyed, limped, neutered, crippled. Answers to the name Lucky." That ad may seem contradictory, but in a larger sense, with all our pain and suffering, with all our discouragement and depression, with our finitude as ever-present background, we are lucky to be alive, to have an opportunity to grow a soul, to share the ministry of pain, to be able to transmute the "eternal severities" into meaning, to live in the embrace of a broken arc.

The Sufi mystic poet Rumi writes,

Come, come whoever you are.
Wanderer, worshipper, lover of leaving,
    come.
Come, though you have broken your vow a
    thousand times.
Ours is not a caravan of despair. Come, yet
    again, come.

Suffering and Meaning: Why Do Bad Things Happen?

Purpose

- To consider the age-old question of human suffering
- To learn how different religions have understood suffering
- To incorporate the meaning of suffering into our credos

Materials

- Copies of Worksheet 10, "Philosophical Statements About Suffering (page 53)," pasted on index cards
- Copy of "The Mustard Seed Medicine" in *From Long Ago and Many Lands* by Sophia Lyon Fahs
- Copies of *Singing the Living Tradition*

Preparation

- Familiarize yourself with Session 8 before the group meets.

SESSION PLAN

Chalice Lighting   5 minutes

Light the chalice and read one or more of the following:

The reasons for living are not withdrawn when life is a broken arc. Following those reasons; get back to the daily tasks; rejoin the circle of friends; remember to serve the people who crave what you, and perhaps you alone, can give. Then you will make a discovery: the loss has not grown less, but life has started anew. Scars remain, but health of spirit equal to the journey has been found.

—Frederick R. Griffin

There is only one thing that I dread: not to be worthy of my suffering.

—Fyodor Dostoyevsky

So it was that when the Hasidic pilgrims vied for who among them had endured the most suffering, who was most entitled to complain, the Zaddik told them the story of the Sorrow Tree. On the Day of Judgment, each person will be allowed to hang all of his unhappiness on a branch of the great Tree of Sorrows. After each person has found a limb from which his own miseries may dangle, they may all walk slowly around the tree. Each is to search for a set of sufferings that he would prefer to those he has hung on the tree. In the end, each man freely chooses to reclaim his own personal set of sorrows rather than those of another. Each man leaves the tree wiser than when he came.

—Sheldon Kopp

Exploring a Personal Philosophy of Suffering   30 minutes

Ask participants to each select a Philosophy of Suffering card at random. Invite them to look back at their answers to question 14 on Worksheet 1, Credo Survey (page xviii), and reflect on the statements they drew.

Discuss:

- How is the statement you drew similar to, or different from, your view of suffering?

- How do you feel about the card you drew?

- Does it correspondent to your own philosophy of suffering?

- Why or why not?

God and Job   45 minutes

This activity may be done with the total group or in small groups of five or six. Dramatize this excerpt from Worksheet 11, The Masque of Reason (page 61), by Robert Frost. Discuss the passage from the point of view of the Philosophy of Suffering cards that participants selected at the beginning of the session. Or invite them to write a short dialogue, individually or with partners, for a play on the "Book of Job Revisited," *ala* Robert Frost. What would Job and God say to each other when reunited?

Alternative:
The Mustard Seed Medicine   45 minutes

As in the God and Job exercise, read the story of "The Mustard Seed Medicine" in *From Long Ago and Many Lands* by Sophia Lyon Fahs and discuss this traditional Buddhist story from the point of view of the "Philosophical Statement About Suffering" card each person is holding.

Alternative:
The Nature of Providence   45 minutes

Read the following passage by John Burroughs to the group:

I see the nature providence going its impartial way.

I see drought and flood, heat and cold, war and pestilence, defeat and death, besetting us at all times in all lands.

I see the elemental forces as indifferent toward us as toward ants and fleas.

I see the righteous defeated and the ungodly triumphant—this and much more I see.

And yet I behold through the immense vista

behind us the human race, slowly—oh so slowly, emerging:

From its brute and semihuman ancestry into the full human estate, from blind instinct and savage passion into consciousness,

I see on an immense scale, and as clearly as in a demonstration in a laboratory, that good comes out of evil;

That the impartiality of the Nature Providence is best;

That we are made strong by what we overcome; that we are human because we are as free to do evil as to do good;

That disease, wars, the unloosened, devastating elemental forces have each and all played their part in developing and hardening us, and giving us the heroic fiber.

Discuss the group's reactions. Do people agree? Why or why not?

Homework for Session 9

- Remind participants to rewrite their credos based on what they have learned in this session and read the Reading for Session 9 (page 62).

Closing Celebration   10 minutes

Invite each member of the group to give a one-sentence sermon on the meaning of suffering to him or her. Read the following.

We have gathered here to walk together as a company of imperfect people seeking a better way. We come wounded in body and spirit, seeking the healing that we can do for one another. It is not easy to wend our ways through the thickets and brambles that beset our paths.

There are temptations to stray from the routes we have planned. There are pitfalls and steep hills and craggy rocks to traverse. There are lesser paths to trod, and dangerous ways to walk.

We are the walking wounded seeking to be healed.

Sometimes we must walk the road alone. In solitary courage we must decide how to travel, and why. Sometimes we are the guides and stay for those who follow.

We seek to mark the paths, still unsure which way to go ourselves.

This we know. It is good to come together to

consider how we walk and with whom. It is good to envision the highest path even as we stagger in the low places. It is good to be with one another in this house of healing, to give and receive the word of encouragement and the helping hand.

Walking this road is never easy, and we need all the help we can get.

For we are the walking wounded, healing one another as we move on an uncertain journey. We are the walking wounded, determined to continue the journey that knows no end.

Close the session by singing "Voice Still and Small," hymn 391 in *Singing the Living Tradition*.

THE MASQUE OF REASON

God: Oh, I remember well: you're Job, my patient.
       How are you now?
       I trust you've quite recovered,
       and feel no ill effects from what I gave you.

Job: Gave me in truth: I like the frank admission . . .

God: I've had you on my mind a thousand years
       To thank you someday for the way you helped me
       Establish once for all the principle
       There's no connection man can reason out
       Between his just deserts and what he gets.
       Virtue may fail and wickedness succeed.
       'Twas a great demonstration we put on.
       . . . Too long I've owed you this apology
       For the apparently unmeaning sorrow
       You were afflicted with in those days.
       But it was of the essence of the trial
       You shouldn't understand it at the time.
       It had to seem unmeaning to have meaning.
       And it came out all right. I have no doubt
       You realize by now the part you played
       To stultify the Deuteronomist
       And change the tenor of religious thought.
       My thanks are to you for releasing me
       From moral bondage to the human race.
       The only free will there at first was man's,
       Who could do good or evil as he chose.
       I had no choice but I must follow him
       With forfeits and rewards he understood—
       Unless I liked to suffer loss of worship.
       I had to prosper good and punish evil.
       You changed all that. You set me free to reign . . .

Job: All very splendid. I am flattered proud
       To have been in on anything with You.
       'Twas a great demonstration if You say so.
       Though incidentally I sometimes wonder
       Why it had to be at my expense.

God: It had to be at somebody's expense.
       Society can never think things out:
       It has to see them acted out by actors,
       Devoted actors at a sacrifice—
       The ablest actors I can lay my hands on . . .

                                         —Robert Frost

Mark Twain had some fun with death. Once, while abroad, he read his obituary in an international newspaper and wrote, "Reports of my death have been greatly exaggerated."

Polish poet Wislawa Szymborska concludes the poem "A Word On Statistics" with these words: "Mortal: one hundred out of one hundred —a figure that has never varied yet."

Death happens. We are, all and each, merely guests of existence.

To dramatize that truth writer Elie Wiesel tells the Hassidic tale of a nineteenth-century tourist from the United States who visits a famous Polish rabbi, Hafez Hayyim. He is astonished to see that the rabbi's home is only a simple room filled with books. A table and a bench are the only furniture.

"Rabbi, where is your furniture?" asks the tourist.

"Where is yours?" replies Hafez.

"Mine? But I'm only a visitor here."

"So am I," says the rabbi.

Only two problems really exist, and neither one can be solved. One of them is life. And the other is death. As Forrest Church puts it,

When we die, everyone else's story goes on, but we are not there to discover how they turn out. . . . But that's the way it is. Our lives stop in the middle. They don't reach a conclusion, they simply stop. The middle of the story is where all our stories end.

On the other hand we can be in denial, so enraptured by our own existence that the prospect of our death is unreal. After all, when we are alive, it is extremely difficult to imagine things happening without our being present to experience them. While this may seem a typical example of youthful exuberance, it also afflicts those of us older souls who are overwhelmed with the wonder of ourselves. We forget the words of playwright Arthur Miller: "Immortality is like trying to carve your initials in a block of ice in the middle of July."

At our most philosophical we may look upon death as a great gift, because it means if we must die then we must be alive. We have life—a great gift though we did nothing at all to deserve it. As Huston Smith writes, "Thanks be for these, for

birth and death; life in between with meaning full; holy becomes the quickened breath; we celebrate life's interval."

In a way we are blessed to be thinking of death and dying. Why? Because that very reflection reminds us of the precious time that has been allotted to us and encourages us to use that interval between birth (over which we had no control) and death (about which we have no choice), and use it wisely. As some wise soul says, "God created time so everything wouldn't happen all at once." We have the opportunity to live our lives not all at once but over a brief but precious interval between two eternities.

If we lived forever, we could constantly postpone everything. As we accept life we accept finitude as part of the bargain. And so death becomes as much a part of life as birth. We are obliged to render something of meaning out of our finite piece of eternity. Length of life does not matter if we cannot create something significant out of our years. Victor Frankl reminds us that if our life is meaningless, it wouldn't take on meaning by becoming eternal.

Elie Wiesel relates the old Hassidic story of a rabbi who is being formally installed in his position. While notables and dignitaries extol his virtues at great length and with excessive eloquence, a strange expression comes over his face.

"What are you thinking of?" the others ask him.

"I have the odd feeling I am attending my own funeral," the rabbi replies.

One of the best ways to understand Unitarian Universalism is to attend our memorial services. We acknowledge death as a natural part of life; we recognize the uniqueness of the deceased; and we remind ourselves that the cycle of living and dying goes on. Often we invite worshipers to speak of the one whose life we have come to celebrate. We share happy and sad stories, anecdotes revealing the best and the not-quite-best of the person. There is laughter; there are tears; the service is in every sense of the word a celebration of life. As J. Donald Johnston tells us, "In the presence of life we say no to death; in the presence of death we say yes to life."

A UU memorial service begins with the words "We light this chalice in memory and in hope." At the conclusion of the service, we say, "We extinguish this flame but not the memory or the hope—they live on in that great mystery of things in which we live and move and have our being." Death is not defeat. Paradoxically it is the culmination of life, that which helps life take on meaning.

The words of the late Roman Catholic priest Henri Nouwen sum it up for us:

> Yes, there is such a thing as a good death. We ourselves are responsible for the way we die. We have to choose between clinging to life in such a way that death becomes nothing but a failure, or letting go of life in freedom, so that we can be given to others as a source of hope. This is a crucial choice, and we have to "work" on that choice every day of our lives. Death does not have to be our final failure, our final defeat in the struggle of life, our unavoidable fate. If our deepest human desire is indeed to give ourselves to others, then we can make our death into a final gift. It is so wonderful to see how fruitful death is when it is a free gift.

Joe Bartlett, a Unitarian Universalist minister and one-time president of Starr King School for the Ministry, inspired many when he wrote of the way in which he accepted his fate. His dying words are memorable: "And with deep satisfaction of my work completed—no gnawing 'might have beens' or guilt that in any but forgivable ways, I've let people down. . . . Yet I feel a certain euphoria. What a launching pad into The Yonder! . . . So this is my farewell to you, to say—yes, really! All is well with me."

Unitarian Universalists tend to have memorial services, without the body present, rather than traditional funerals, so we might focus on the spiritual more than the physical. It might be interesting to write a service for yourself as if you were attending—and you will be, in a way—and indicate what you would like to hear. A similar experience might come from writing one's own epitaph or obituary. While these exercises might seem a trifle odd, they are powerfully value-clarifying experiences. Why?

Sometimes we are so close to the details of daily living we cannot see our lives whole. When we imagine ourselves at our own memorial service, living takes on a new dimension. We begin to realize we are not going to be here forever; what we wish to make of our lives we had better do, if we have not done so already. We see ourselves as others see

us—if only in imagination. We sort out the consequential from the trivial. This perspective is harder to find in the crush and rush of daily routines.

Take the case of Alfred Nobel, the Swedish chemist and industrialist who once had the life-changing experience of reading his own obituary. His brother had died, but a Paris report made a mistake in reporting the death of the "dynamite king." Nobel awoke to find his life laid out on the front page of his morning paper. The shock was overwhelming and life changing. From the report, it would have seemed that death, destruction, the arms trade, and money were his life. Nobel had a kinder view of himself, but this was ignored. He was, to the public, simply a merchant of death, the dynamite king. Nobel resolved to make clear to the world the true meaning and purpose of his life. He devised a plan to dispose of his fortune so that it might support individuals and groups who are effective in working for understanding and peace. The Nobel Prizes, then, were born from a mistaken obituary.

In Mitch Albom's *Tuesdays with Morrie*, Professor Morrie Schwartz, who is dying of Lou Gehrig's disease, returns disappointed from a colleague's funeral at Brandeis University. "What a waste," he says. "All those people saying all those wonderful things, and Irv never got to hear any of it." And so he made some calls and set a date, and on a cold Sunday afternoon he and a small group of friends and family had a "living funeral" —for him. As Albom describes the event,

> Each of them spoke and paid tribute to my old professor. Some cried. Some laughed. Morrie cried and laughed with them. And all the heartfelt things we never get to say to those we love, Morrie said that day. His 'living funeral' was a rousing success.

One devout Christian, dying of Alzheimer's disease, writes,

> The greatest fear I have is what this disease does to your personality. It can make you angry, ugly, obscene, paranoid, cursing, and very difficult to handle before you become comatose. Pray that I be spared part of this personality change. Pray that I in no way inadvertently disgrace the Lord, this church, or the people whom I love. Pray for Betty (his wife) as I turn guardianship over to her. I will not suffer nearly as much as she will.

. . . And please have patience with me. . . . Please remember me the way I was.

Who are we anyway? What is our essence? Are we what we are now? Or what we have been? One day we will be at the last stage. Let us remember, let everyone remember that our lives are not simply what we are at the moment, for good or ill. We are the sum of the parts of an entire life. Please remember us the way we were.

Our mortality is tenuous. We are but guests of existence, brief visitors upon this earth. Many of us are agnostic about immortality. We do not know. We try not to be in denial about our mortality. Woody Allen writes about death,

> It's not that I'm afraid to die. I just don't want to be there when it happens. . . . Death is nature's way of telling us to slow down. . . . Some people want to achieve immortality through their works or their descendents. I prefer to achieve immortality by not dying. . . . I do not believe in an afterlife, although I am bringing a change of underwear.

As Alan Watts says, "No one imagines that a symphony is supposed to improve in quality as it goes along, or that the whole object of playing it is to reach the finale. The point of music is discovered in every moment of playing and listening to it."

Each moment of life is an event worthy in and of itself. Death points to the precious quality of each instant. Some among us believe in a mystical kind of immortality—a spiritual existence beyond death. Some believe in a kind of biological immortality—our ashes will help nourish the earth. Some believe in influential immortality—as the stone thrown into the pond causes ripples that reach the farthest shore, something of what we are and do will never be lost.

Some of us do not believe in personal immortality, some conscious existence beyond death. If we're wrong, there surely is no better way to prepare for it than living this life as if it is all we'll get.

In one sense we are always preparing for our memorial service—not as an event but as a reminder that while life can be understood backwards, it is lived forwards. We have the benefit of time to do a summing up, a life review. We have the opportunity to create an "ethical will"—a legacy of words and deeds far more important than our material leavings. We have the luxury of contemplating that celebration of our lives without expecting it to be right around the corner—but who knows? This exercise in spiritual imagination challenges us to deeper and better living. The prospect of our own memorial service greatly concentrates our minds. Contemplation of death greatly intensifies our experience of life.

And so as we face up to our inevitable demise, we say not "please, more"—but "thank you for so much." Perhaps as we consider attending our own memorial services, contemplating how we wish to be remembered, we will be prompted to live so well, as Mark Twain says, "that even the undertaker will be sorry."

Resources on Death

Grollman, Earl A. *Living When a Loved One Has Died*. Boston: Beacon Press, 1995.

Kübler Ross, Elisabeth. *Death—The Final Stage of Growth*. Englewood Cliffs, NJ: Prentice Hall, 1975.

Kübler Ross, Elisabeth. *On Death and Dying*. New York: Macmillan, 1969.

Lamont, Corliss. *A Humanist Funeral Service*. Buffalo: Prometheus Books, 1977.

Lamont, Corliss. *Man Answers Death*. New York: Philosophical Library, 1959.

Marshall, George. *Facing Death and Grief*. Buffalo: Prometheus Books, 1981.

Morgan, Ernest. *A Manual of Death Education and Simple Burial*. Burnsville, NC: The Celo Press, 1980.

Partnow, Elaine, ed. *The Quotable Woman*. Los Angeles: Pinnacle Books, 1977.

Seaburg, Carl, Ed. *Great Occasions*. Boston: Skinner House, 1998, pp. 159–409.

Silliman, Vincent B. *A Selection of Services for Special Occasions*. Boston: UUMA, 1981.

Silliman, Vincent B., ed. *We Sing of Life with We Speak of Life*. Boston: Beacon Press, 1955.

Simmons, Philip. *Learning to Fall: The Blessings of an Imperfect Life*. New York: Bantam Books, 2000.

Smith, Bradford. *Dear Gift of Life: A Man's Encounter with Death*. Wallingford, PA: Pendle Hill Publications, 1965.

Tolstoy, Leo. "The Death of Ivan Ilytch," from *Religion from Tolstoy to Camus*, Walter Kaufman, ed. New York: Harper and Row, 1961.

Unitarian Universalist Association. *Hymns for the Celebration of Life*. Boston: Beacon Press, 1964

Unitarian Universalist Association. *Singing the Living Tradition*. Boston: Beacon Press, 1993.

Voss, Carl Herman, ed. *Quotations of Vision and Courage*. New York: Association Press, 1972.

Death and Immortality: How Do We Celebrate Life?

Purpose

- To learn the beliefs about death and immortality of various religious and cultural traditions
- To explore feelings on death and immortality
- To create our own memorial services

Materials

- Copies of *Singing the Living Tradition*
- Any or all of the Resources on Death on page 64. Participants may also know of alternate selections.
- Copies of *Old Tales for a New Day* by Sophia Lyon Fahs and Alice Cobb

Preparation

- Familiarize yourself with Session 9 before the group meets.
- Print the following questions on newsprint: "What is your understanding of the meaning of suffering?" and "How do you believe death fits into the human condition?"

SESSION PLAN

Chalice Lighting   5 minutes

Light the chalice and read one or more of the following:

> Death? Why this fuss about death? Use your imagination, try to visualize a world without death!
>
> —Charlotte Perkins Gilman

> You are anxious about whether you will rise from the dead or not, but you rose from the dead when you were born and you didn't notice.
>
> —Boris Pasternak

> I would like to believe when I die that I have given myself away like a tree that sows seeds every spring and never counts the loss, because it is not loss, it is adding to future life. It is the tree's way of being. Strongly rooted perhaps, but spilling out its treasure on the wind.
>
> —May Sarton

> I regard the heaven and earth as my coffin and outer coffin, the sun and the moon as a pair of jade gifts and the constellations as my burial jewels. And the whole creation shall come to my funeral. Will it not be a grand funeral? What more should I want?
>
> —Lao-tse

> Watching a peaceful death of a human being reminds us of a falling star; one of the million stars in a vast sky that flares up for the brief moment only to disappear into the endless night forever.
>
> —Elisabeth Kübler-Ross

A Liberal Religious Understanding of Death   15 minutes

Show participants the two questions on newsprint. What are the options for beliefs about death and immortality? Discuss each question in turn. Ask participants to write brief personal statements on their own views of death and immortality.

Planning Memorial Services   60 minutes

This activity is purposely placed near the end of the seminar with the hope that the group will have developed a trust level that will make it possible to share deeply personal responses to life and death. Discussing one's own demise and memorial service may be emotionally difficult. You may want to invite a guest skilled in helping people work through the subject of death and dying if there is no such person in the group. Someone familiar to all or most of the group members would be preferable to an unknown counselor.

Ask participants to draw a line on a piece of paper, writing their birth date to the left and their projected date of death to the right. Then ask them to place a mark on the line to represent today.

Discuss:

- How do you feel about that mark's placement?

- What do you plan to do between now and the date on the right?

- How does that make you feel?

There seems to be general agreement that a dignified memorial service suits our needs better than a traditional funeral, although there is doubtless debate on this point. For the purposes of this exercise, let's focus on a memorial service, which has three purposes: to acknowledge the death of the loved one as part of the natural processes of creation, to celebrate the life of the deceased, to inspire survivors to go back into the routines of their days with hope and courage. These purposes may suggest the outline for a memorial service. The service may consist of readings, prayer, meditations, eulogies, and music, among other elements. Ask participants to create the memorial services that they might like to have upon their deaths. They can be written out in some detail or simply outlined. Refer participants to the resources you brought.

Invite people to share their services in small groups or in the total group and discuss:

- Why did you make the choices you did?

- How would you frame your eulogy?

Alternative:
Writing Your Obituary   30 minutes

Invite participants to try writing their own obituaries in any way they wish. This can be a powerful experience. Share these thoughts to get them started:

> To the Indian the primary goal of creative energy is the creation of energy within the individual. This is why an Indian will work with complete absorption and with utter concentration upon a sand painting that must be destroyed as the sun sets. He knows his work as a concrete product will vanish with the single day, but the healing that it has accomplished will live again, a re-creation, and all who have participated in this ceremony will have shared in the creation and rebirth of power.
> —Frances G. Wickes, "The Creative Process"

> We're back, we've all come back;
> We've all been given a longer time
> To look and touch and love.
> —John Haynes Holmes

Alternative:
Writing an Ethical Will   30 minutes

Ethical wills are an increasing trend. This kind of will passes along spiritual insights rather than material wealth. Encourage participants to think about their ethical wills. How would they sum up a lifetime of learning? An ethical will is a living legacy of the intangible. Here is one example that you can read to the group to prime the pump:

I wish you well, my friends, in the impossible possibility of living the good life.
Let what you are speak more loudly than what you say.
Let your very being craft a silent sermon that needs no words.
Maintain and cherish your integrity in the struggle to be good and do rightly.
Let the inner and the outer person be as one so that your doing flows as a fountain from your being.
Have faith that if the soul is pure, the hands will do rightly.
Risk being for others and forgive yourself when you cannot.

Let neither reward nor punishment, neither fear of hell nor lure of heaven, distract you from your earthly tasks.

Finally, so you will not take yourself nor the awesome task of the good life too seriously, I offer this advice:

Always be a little kinder than necessary.

Do unto others 20 percent better than you would have them do unto you to correct for subjective error.

Shalom.

Alternative: Death and Immortality in Different Cultures   30 minutes

Form small groups for this activity, or have individuals choose one of the following stories from *Old Tales for a New Day* by Sophia Lyon Fahs and Alice Cobb and report on the view of death and immortality expressed:

- "Brahman, the Universal Being" (What does it mean to live forever?) from the Hindu tradition, pp. 189–193.

- "Mawu's Ways Are Best" (Why does everybody have to die?) from Benin, Africa, pp. 173–177.

- "The Soldier Dreams" (When you die, is that the end of you?) from the Buddhist tradition, pp. 178–180.

- "Mpobe, the Hunter" (Where do people go when they die?) from Uganda, Africa, pp. 181–184.

- "The King's Question" (What will we be like after we die?) from the Buddhist tradition, pp. 185–188.

Homework for Session 10

- Ask participants to complete Worksheet 12, A Catechism for Unitarian Universalists (page 69).

- Remind participants to rewrite their credos based on what they have learned in this session and read the Reading for Session 10 (page 71).

Closing Celebration   10 minutes

Invite each person to read a brief selection of her or his own choosing or writing, and ask the group to respond with "Amen" after each reading. Sing hymn 322, "Thanks Be for These," or one of the hymns in the "Grief and Loss" or "Death and Life" section of *Singing the Living Tradition.*

A CATECHISM FOR UNITARIAN UNIVERSALISTS

Traditionally a catechism is a manual of instruction, in question-and-answer form, for indoctrination into a particular system of faith and morals. In our creedless faith, a catechism would be an anathema. It may well be that how we believe is more important than what we believe, that the process is our most important product. Yet taken too this can mean abdication from the task of creating any faith at all. Thus, you are invited to do a catechism in progress, using the questions suggested below or those of your own formulation and answering them succinctly.

1. What is religion?

2. What does *Universalism* mean?

3. What does *Unitarianism* mean?

4. What is the meaning of Jesus for Unitarian Universalists?

5. Do you believe in the Resurrection? Explain.

6. Is there life after death? Explain.

7. What about heaven and hell? Explain.

8. Do you believe in salvation, then? If so, what is it?

9. What about human nature? Do you believe in original sin?

10. Do you believe in sin at all? Explain.

11. What is your idea of Ultimate Reality?

12. What is your source of authority in religion?

13. What do you believe about the Bible as a source of truth?

14. Are you a Christian or not? Why?

15. What is the meaning of life for a Unitarian Universalist?

READING FOR SESSION 10

Now, for the final session of this program, we consider what it might mean to have a "Spiritual Check-Up." Beliefnet sponsors an online religious inventory. Here is their interpretation of the scores:

25–29: Hardcore Skeptic—but interested or you wouldn't be here!

30–39: Spiritual Dabbler—open to spiritual matters but far from impressed

40–49: Active Spiritual Seeker—spiritual but turned off by organized religion

50–59: Spiritual Straddler—one foot in traditional religion, one foot in free-form spirituality

60–69: Old-fashioned Seeker—happy with your religion but searching for the right expression of it

70–79: Questioning Believer—you have doubts about the particulars but not the Big Stuff.

80–89: Confident Believer—you have little doubt you've found the right path.

90–100: Candidate for Clergy.

One student of spirituality cites the symptoms of spiritual health:

- a tendency to think and act spontaneously rather than from fears based on past experience

- an unmistakable ability to enjoy each moment

- a loss of interest in judging other people

- a loss of interest in interpreting the actions of others

- a loss of interest in conflict

- a loss of ability to worry (this is a very serious symptom!)

- frequent and overwhelming episodes of appreciation

- contented feelings of connectedness with people, places, and things—especially with nature

- frequent attacks of smiling

- an increasing tendency to let things happen, rather than trying to make them happen

- an increased susceptibility to the love extended by others, as well as the uncontrollable urge to extend it

In Unitarian Universalism we do not give out spiritual report cards. That would be an act of presumption. It is not a bad idea, however, to undertake a periodic self-examination.

The question is not "how are you feeling?" but "how's your soul?" or spirit or psyche?

Spirituality is one of those squishy words. The more you try to define what you're talking about, the more elusive it becomes. We enter the dangerous and mysterious world of the intangible, the subjective. Being spiritual has been likened to "nailing down the air in a balloon." *Spirit* in Latin means "to breathe"; in the Hebrew scriptures it is life, breath, *ruah*; in the Christian scriptures it is *pneuma*, life force, vitality, and aliveness. The spiritual realm has to do with the invisible forces that create and sustain life, the very ground of our being. It is the inner dimension of things.

Unitarian Universalists would do well to attempt a personal and communal spiritual check-up, consisting more of stories than of facts, more of questions than of answers. Diagnosis and prescription will not be high-tech. Pablo Picasso says, "Computers are useless; they can only give you answers." Spirituality is more art than science. Oliver Wendell Holmes writes that "life is painting a picture, not doing a sum."

Learning to ask the right questions is crucial. A certain cartoon aptly sums up our dilemma. It pictures a large and impressive building, The Research Institute, with two signs at the entrance, pointing in opposite directions: In one direction the sign reads "unanswered questions" and in the other direction "unquestioned answers."

We make the assumption here that spirituality is a lot like health; we may have good health or poor health, but health itself is something we can't avoid. The same is true of spirituality: every human being is a spiritual being. The question is not whether we 'have spirituality' but whether the spirituality we have is a negative one that leads to isolation and self-destruction or one that is more positive and life-giving."

With our spiritual stethoscopes at the ready then, we ask each other and ourselves, "How are you feeling, spiritually?"

When you get out of bed in the morning, are you glad to be alive? Or like one of Charles Schultz's Peanut's characters do you "dread one day at a time"? When you go to bed at night, are you relieved that the day is over, or do you give thanks for yet another day of living?

Zest for living is a key spiritual health indicator. The word *enthusiasm* derives from the Greek for an extravagant religious emotion, literally possession by a god. Kathleen Norris writes in her "spiritual geography" *Dakota,*

Two women I know were diagnosed with terminal cancer. One said, "If I ever get out of this hospital, I'm going to look out for Number One. " And that's exactly what she did. Against overwhelming odds, she survived, and it made her mean.

The other woman spoke about the blessings of a life that had taken some hard blows: her mother had killed herself when she was a girl, her husband had died young. I happened to visit her just after she'd been told that she had less than a year to live. She was dry-eyed, and had been reading the Psalms. She was entirely realistic about her illness and said to me, "The one thing that scares me is the pain. I hope I die before I turn into an old bitch." I told her family that story after the funeral, and they loved it; they could hear in it their mother's voice, the way she really was.

One's attitude in facing each day is indicative of spiritual health or illness. As poet Stephen Dunn writes, "To have any chance at a good life—a friend once said in a letter—you have to keep saying abracadabra even though nothing happens."

Do you have a healthy sense of humor about yourself and the contradictions, paradoxes, and oxymorons of life? When in doubt, can you laugh at life?

In recalling her early life on the prairie, Kathleen

Norris notes her fundamentalist upbringing and her vision of a "Monster God":

My uncle told me once about having his mother sit at the edge of his bed and tell him that Jesus might come as a thief in the night and tomorrow could be that great day when the world ends.

"That sucks when you'd been planning a ball game and a rubber gun battle," he said. He would pull the covers over his head when she left, and try to shut out the sounds of Jesus sneaking around in the dark.

If you take yourself too seriously, the doctor cannot give you a clean bill of health.

Can you deal with the inevitable tragedies of life, including death, even your own?

Mary Catherine Bateson tells of her life with parents Margaret Mead and Gregory Bateson and how they chose to die after they were both diagnosed with cancer:

Though she had always insisted that life should include an acknowledgment of death, Margaret refused, in the face of incontrovertible evidence, to admit she was dying and engaged a 'healer' to treat her. Gregory died a planned death, surrounded by Zen students meditating day and night.

A reviewer of Bateson's memoir concludes, "When the time came, neither of these world-famous scientists, it seems, found knowledge or rationality much help in facing the unknown."

Like how we live our life, how we face our death is an indicator of spiritual health. Religion prepares us for the worst, as well as the best, that life offers.

Do you manifest your spirituality in the world so that people take inspiration from who and what you are?

One member of an adult program class in "Writing Your Spiritual Autobiography" writes that spirituality is

the deepest inner core of my being; the source of inner strength, of endurance, of meaning, of awe; the life force that keeps me wanting to grow, to learn, to create, to change, to relate, and to love; my own unique bit of DNA, that at the same time connects me to the Life Force of the entire universe; that stores up inspiration from nature, from all kinds of other people, and from all kinds of art forms; and that helps me to get through the hard things.

Does your faith overflow into service?

Kathleen Norris gives a poignant and moving account of her little church on the plains, Hope Church, Presbyterian, at which she served as occasional lay preacher:

> Hope Church gives the people who live around it a sense of identity. Hope is well cared for. Both the outhouse and the sanctuary are freshly painted. As one pastor recently put it, the thing that makes Hope so vibrant is that the congregation is so alive to the world. They conducted a study of the politics of hunger. In recent hard times, while Hope's membership declined by nearly half, the amount the church donates for mission has increased every year. It now ranks near the top in per capita giving among Presbyterian churches in the state of South Dakota. One former pastor said, "It can be astonishing how tiny Hope Church makes you feel so strongly that you're part of a global entity."

Vibrant spirituality and social responsibility are a seamless web in which our gratitude for being overflows into service.

Does your spirituality lift you and your life into larger frameworks of meaning so that you see your life as a worthy project, so that you take joy in the work of your hands and heart?

For thirty-five years Paul Cezanne lived in obscurity, producing masterpieces that he gave away to unsuspecting neighbors. So great was his love for his work that he never gave a thought to achieving recognition, nor did he suspect that someday he would be looked upon as the father of modern painting. Cezanne owes his first fame to a Paris art dealer who chanced upon his paintings, put some of them together, and presented the world of art with the first Cezanne exhibition. The world was astonished to discover the pres-

ence of a master. The master was just as astonished. Shortly after the exhibition opened, Cezanne, arriving at the gallery leaning on the arm of his son, could not contain his amazement when he saw his paintings on display. Turning to his son he exclaimed, "Look, they have framed them!"

We all need to have the work of our lives framed in some larger context than the everyday. That is spiritual health.

Does your spiritual health enable you to celebrate life?

In an interview with the television journalist Bill Moyers, mythology scholar Joseph Campbell tells a captivating story about ringing the great bronze bell at Chartres Cathedral:

> I consider Chartres my parish. I've been there often. When I was a student in Paris, I spent one whole weekend in the cathedral, studying every single figure there. I was there so much that the concierge came up to me one noontime and said, "Would you like to go up with me and ring the bells?" I said, "I sure would." So we climbed the tower up to the great bronze bell. There was a little platform like a seesaw. He stood on one end of the seesaw, and I stood on the other end of the seesaw, and there was a little bar there for us to hold on to. He gave the thing a push, and then he was on it, and I was on it. And we started going up and down, and the wind was blowing through our hair, up there in the cathedral, and then it began ringing underneath us—"bong, bong, bong." It was one of the most thrilling adventures of my life. When it was over, he brought me down, and he said, "I want to show you where my room is." Well, in a cathedral you have the nave, then the transept, and then the apse, and around the apse is the choir screen. He took me through a little door in the middle of the choir screen, and there was his little bed and a little table with a lamp on it. When I looked out through the screen, there was the window of the Black Madonna—and that was where he lived. Now, there was a man living by constant meditation. That was a moving, beautiful thing. I've been to Chartres time and time again since.

A Spiritual Check-Up: Where Do We Go from Here?

Purpose

- To provide closure for the group experience
- To provide a way to share credos in progress
- To afford opportunity for further experiences of religious learning and growth

Materials

- Copies of *Singing the Living Tradition*

Preparation

- Familiarize yourself with Session 10 before the group meets.

SESSION PLAN

Chalice Lighting   5 minutes

Light the chalice and read one or more of the following:

All my life I wanted to be somebody, but I should have been more specific.

—Lily Tomlin

I cannot myself raise the winds that might blow us to a safe harbor, but I can at least raise the sails so that when the wind does come I can catch it.

—E. F. Schumacher

We are a stream whose source is hidden. . . . The soul knows only the soul; the web of events is the flowing robe in which she is clothed.

—Ralph Waldo Emerson

As for "spirituality," that contemporary code word of gaseous, noncommittal religion, that evasive term that may refer to little more than a warm tingle in the toes.

—Martin Marty

People say that what we're all seeking is a meaning for life. I don't think that's what we're really seeking. I think that what we're seeking is an experience of being alive, so that our life experiences on the purely physical plane will have resonances within our own innermost being and reality, so that we actually feel the rapture of being alive.

—Joseph Campbell

I used to think we live on a human plane and possess a spiritual life, which we are responsible for tending. . . . I now believe that I live on a spiritual plane and possess a human life. What this means, quite simply, is that every moment I am alive I am living my spirituality.

—Denise Tracy

So today I am more comfortable talking about the experience of the sacred than about the existence of a divine being.

—Bob Mesle

Our inner weather marks what is essential in us.
It signifies the workings of the spirit.
It measures the meaning of our lives.
It marks the rites of passage through which we move.
It celebrates those tiny triumphs of the soul we cherish.

It moves us to heights of ecstasy,
And sustains us in depths of despair.
It shelters us in moments of loss
And supports us when we are sore distressed.
It enables us to endure and to prevail
When life seems only to buffet and rebuff us.
It helps us understand the mysteries that sur-
round us
And praise the majesty in which we live.
Behold our inner weather—the workings of
the spirit—
May we embrace it, relish it, celebrate it all
year round.

—Richard S. Gilbert

I determine to live the outer life in the inward sanctuary. The outer life must find its meaning, the source of its strength in the inward sanctuary. As this is done, the gulf between outer and inner will narrow and my life will be increasingly whole and of one piece. What I do in the outer will be blessed by the holiness of the inward sanctuary; for indeed it shall all be one.

—Howard Thurman

Unitarian Universalist Catechism   20 minutes

Discuss the completed UU catechism:

- Does the idea of a UU catechism disturb you?

- How does a catechism differ from a creed or a credo?

Credo Sharing   45 minutes

Invite each person to share a favorite section of his or her credo as a way to bring closure to the group experience.

Evaluation   5 minutes

Invite the group members to assess their experience as participants in this seminar. The Feedback Sheet may be a useful tool to help the group recall the various sections of the seminar. Send the completed evaluation sheets to the UUA Faith Development Staff Group, 25 Beacon Street, Boston, MA 02108.

Unfinished Business   5 minutes

Ask the group whether there there were issues raised during the group sessions that were not resolved or that need further clarification or attention? The group may choose those issues it wishes to address in the remaining minutes of the session, or perhaps the group might like to continue to meet on a monthly basis.

Closing Celebration   10 minutes

Rabbi Akiba, the "father of Rabbinic Judaism," was once asked to recite the essence of the law while standing on one foot. Ask each person in the group to distill the essence of his or her own theology into one sentence. This is sometimes known as the "elevator speech."

Read one of the above passages, share any final thoughts, and join hands to sing "Spirit of Life," hymn 123 in *Singing the Living Tradition.*

Resources

Adams, James Luther. *On Being Human Religiously*. Boston: Beacon Press, 1976.

Adams, James Luther, and Hiltner, Seward, eds. *Pastoral Care in the Liberal Churches*. Nashville: Abingdon Press, 1970.

Alexander, Scott W., ed., *Everyday Spiritual Practice: Simple Pathways for Enriching Your Life*. Boston: Skinner House Books, 1999.

Allport, Gordon. *Becoming*. New Haven: Yale University Press, 1955.

Barth, Joseph. "The State of the Unitarian Universalist Churches and Their Ministry." A Minns Lecture by Joseph Barth, October 5, 1975.

Beach, George Kimmich, ed. *The Essential James Luther Adams*. Boston: Skinner House Books, 1998.

_____ . *Transforming Liberalism: The Theology of James Luther Adams*. Boston: Skinner House Books, 2005.

Berger, Peter. *A Rumor of Angels*. Garden City: Doubleday & Co., 1969.

Buber, Martin. *To Hallow This Life*, edited by Jacob Trapp. New York: Harper and Brothers, 1958.

Campbell, Joseph, with Bill Moyers. *The Power of Myth*. New York: Doubleday, 1988.

Cavafy, C. P. *The Complete Poems of Cavafy*. Orlando, FL: Harcourt, Brace, Jovanovich, Inc., 1949.

Chodron, Pema. *When Things Fall Apart: Heart Advice for Difficult Times*. Boston: Shambhala, 1997.

Clinebell, Howard J., Jr., "Mental Health Through the Religious Community" *Pastoral Psychology*, Vol. 20, No. 194, May 1969.

Commission on Appraisal. *Engaging Our Theological Diversity*. Boston: Unitarian Universalist Association, 2005.

Cousineau, Phil, ed., *Soul: An Archaeology*. San Francisco: HarperSanFrancisco, 1994.

Erikson, Erik. *Childhood and Society*. New York: W. W. Norton & Company, 1950.

Fahs, Sophia Lyon, ed. *From Long Ago and Many Lands: Stories for Children Told Anew*. Second edition. Boston: Skinner House Books, 1995.

Fahs, Sophia Lyon. *Worshipping Together With Questioning Minds*. Boston: Beacon Press, 1965.

Fahs, Sophia Lyon, and Cobb, Alice. *Old Tales for a New Day*. Buffalo: Prometheus Books, 1980.

Fahs, Sophia Lyon, and Spoerl, Dorothy T. *Beginnings of Earth, Sky, Life, Death*. Boston: Beacon Press, revised edition Starr King Press, 1958.

Fowler, James W. *Becoming Adult Becoming Christian: Adult Development and Christian Faith*. San Francisco: Jossey-Bass Publishers, 2000.

Frankl, Viktor. *Man's Search for Meaning.* Reprint ed. Boston: Beacon Press, 2000.

Fromm, Erich. *Psychoanalysis and Religion.* New Haven: Yale University Press, 1950.

Fromm, Erich. *You Shall Be As Gods: A Radical Interpretation of the Old Testament and Its Tradition.* New York: Holt, Rinehart and Winston, 1966.

Frost, Edward A., ed. *With Purpose and Principle: Essays about the Seven Principles of Unitarian Universalism.* Boston: Skinner House Books, 1998.

Frost, Robert. *Complete Poems of Robert Frost.* New York: Holt, Rinehart and Winston, 1964.

Fulfilling the Promise Committee. Final report to General Assembly, 2001. Available at www.uua.org/ga/ga01/4015.html.

Gilbert, Richard S. *Building Your Own Theology, Volume 1: Introduction.* Boston: Unitarian Universalist Association, 2000.

_____ . *Building Your Own Theology, Volume 3: Ethics.* Boston: Unitarian Universalist Association, 1994.

_____ . *The Prophetic Imperative: The Social Gospel in Theory and Practice.* Boston: Unitarian Universalist Association, 2001.

Great Dialogues of Plato. New York: Mentor Books, The New American Library, 1956.

Grodzins, Dean, ed. *A Language of Reverence.* Chicago: Meadville Lombard Press, 2004.

Grollman, Earl A. *Living When a Loved One Has Died.* Boston: Beacon Press, 1995.

Gustafson, James. *Theology and Christian Ethics.* Philadelphia: United Church Press, 1974.

Halverson, Marvin, and Cohen, Arthur A., eds. *A Handbook of Christian Theology.* New York: Meridian Books, 1958.

Hammarskjold, Dag. *Markings.* London: Faber and Faber, 1964.

Hayward, Jack. *Existentialism and Liberal Religion.* Boston: Beacon Press, 1962.

Heyward, Carter. *The Redemption of God.* Washington, D.C.: University Press of America, 1982.

Hill, Robert L. *The Complete Guide to Small Group Ministry: Saving the World Ten at a Time.* Boston: Skinner House Books, 2003.

Iron, Paul. *A Manual and Guide for Those Who Conduct a Humanist Funeral Service.* Baltimore: Waverly Press, 1971.

Jones, William. *Is God a White Racist? A Preamble to Black Theology.* Boston: Beacon Press, 1998.

Jung, Carl. *Answer to Job.* London: Routledge & Kegan Paul, 1954.

Kierkegaard, Soren. *A Kierkegaard Anthology*, ed. by Robert Bretall. New York: Modern Library, 1946.

Kübler-Ross, Elisabeth. *Death—The Final Stage of Growth.* Englewood Cliffs, NJ: Prentice Hall, 1975.

_____ . *On Death and Dying.* New York: Macmillan, 1969.

Kurtz, Paul, ed. *Humanist Manifestos I and II.* Buffalo, NY: Prometheus Books, 1973.

Lao-tse, *The Wisdom of Lao-tse.* New York: Modern Library, 1948.

Lamont, Corliss. *A Humanist Funeral Service.* Buffalo: Prometheus Books, 1977.

_____ . *Man Answers Death.* New York: Philosophical Library, 1959.

Marshall, George. *Facing Death and Grief.* Buffalo: Prometheus Books, 1981.

Maslow, Abraham. *The Farther Reaches of Human Nature.* New York: The Viking Press, 1971.

Menninger, Karl. *Whatever Became of Sin?* New York: Hawthorne Books, 1973.

Meserve, Harry. *The Practical Meditator*, New York: Human Sciences Press, 1981.

Miller, Robert L. H. *Review of Religious Research.* Vol. 17: No. 3 (Spring, 1976).

Morgan, Ernest. *A Manual of Death Education and Simple Burial*. Burnsville, NC: The Celo Press, 1980.

Muir, Fredric John. *Heretic's Faith: Vocabulary for Religious Liberals*. Boston: Skinner House Books, 2001.

Murray, William R. *A Faith for All Seasons: Liberal Religion and the Crises of Life*. Bethesda, MD: River Road Press, 1990.

Norris, Kathleen. *Dakota: A Spiritual Geography*. New York: Ticknor & Fields, 1993.

_____ . *The Cloister Walk*. New York: Riverhead Books, 1996.

Owen-Towle, Tom. *Freethinking Mystics with Hands: Exploring the Heart of Unitarian Universalism*. Boston: Skinner House Books, 1998.

Patton, Kenneth. *Hymns of Humanity*. Ridgewood, NJ: Meeting House Press, 1980.

Pennick, Nigel. *The Pagan Book of Days: A Guide to the Festivals, Traditions and Sacred Days of the Year*. Rochester, Vermont. Destiny Books, 1992.

Partnow, Elaine, ed. *The Quotable Woman*. Los Angeles: Pinnacle Books, 1977.

Rahtjen, Bruce D., *Experiential Theology*. Kansas City, MO: Associates in Experiential Theology, 1977.

Rasor, Paul. *Faith Without Certainty: Liberal Theology in the 21st Century*. Boston: Skinner House Books, 2005.

Richardson, Robert D., Jr., *Henry Thoreau: A Life of the Mind*. Berkeley: University of California Press, 1986.

Schulz, William. *Making the Manifesto: The Birth of Religious Humanism*. Boston: Skinner House Books, 2002.

Seaburg, Carl, ed. *Great Occasions*. Boston: Skinner House, 1998.

Seaburg, Carl, ed. *The Communion Book*. Boston: Unitarian Universalist Ministers Association, 1993.

Silliman, Vincent B. *A Selection of Services for Special Occasions*. Boston: UUMA, 1981.

Silliman, Vincent B., ed. *We Sing of Life with We Speak of Life*. Boston: Beacon Press, 1955.

Simmons, Philip. *Learning to Fall: The Blessings of an Imperfect Life*. New York: Bantam Books, 2000.

Simon, Sidney, Howe, Leland, W., and Kirschenbaum, Howard. *Values Clarification*. New York: Hart Publishing Co., 1972.

Smith, Bradford. *Dear Gift of Life: A Man's Encounter with Death*. Wallingford, PA: Pendle Hill Publications, 1965.

Smith, Huston. *The World's Religions*. San Francisco: HarperSanFrancisco, 1991.

Tapp, Robert. *Religion Among the Unitarian Universalists: Converts in the Stepfather's House*. Boston: Unitarian Universalist Association, 1973.

Tao Te Ching. Gia-Fu Feng and Jane English, tr. New York: Vintage Books (Random House), 1972.

Tillich, Paul. *The New Being*. New York: Charles Scribner's Sons, 1955.

Tolstoy, Leo. "The Death of Ivan Ilytch," from *Religion from Tolstoy to Camus*, Walter Kaufman, ed. New York: Harper and Row, 1961.

Trapp, Jacob. *The Light of a Thousand Suns*. New York: Harper and Row, 1973.

Unitarian Universalist Association. *Hymns for the Celebration of Life*. Boston: Beacon Press, 1964.

Unitarian Universalist Association. *Singing the Living Tradition*. Boston: Beacon Press, 1993.

Unitarian Universalist Association. *The Free Church in a Changing World*. Boston: UUA, 1963.

Unitarian Universalist Association. "Unitarian Universalist Views of Science and Religion," Boston: UUA pamphlet.

Unitarian Universalist Association. "Unitarian Universalist Views of Suffering." Boston: UUA pamphlet.

UUA Commission on Appraisal. *Belonging: The Meaning of Membership*. Boston: Unitarian Universalist Association, 2001.

UUA Commission on Appraisal. *Interdependence: Renewing Congregational Polity*. Boston: Unitarian Universalist Association, 1997.

Unitarian Universalist Ministers Association. Convocation 1975: *What Is Humanness? What Is Church? What Is Ministry?* Boston: UUMA/LREDA, Brandoch L. Lovely, ed.

Voss, Carl Herman, ed. *Quotations of Vision and Courage*. New York: Association Press, 1972.

Voss, Carl Herman. *The Universal God*. Boston: Beacon Press, 1953.

Whitehead, Alfred North. *Religion in the Making*. New York: Meridian Books, 1960.

Wieman, Henry Nelson, "The Dynamics of Worship." Boston, UUA pamphlet 1979.

Wolfe, Roland Emerson. *Men of Prophetic Fire*. Boston: Beacon Press, 1951.

Wright, Conrad. *Walking Together: Polity and Participation in Unitarian Universalist Churches*. Boston: Skinner House Books, 1989.

Zinn, Howard. *You Can't Be Neutral on a Moving Train: A Personal History of Our Times*. Boston: Skinner House Books, 1995.

Evaluation

We welcome your critique of this program and suggestions. Please share your honest responses on the form below and send it to:

Faith Development Office
Attention: Curricula
Unitarian Universalist Association
24 Farnsworth St., Boston, MA 02210-1409

Introduction

Session 1: Truth and Authority: What Do We Know for Sure?

Session 2: Unity in Diversity: What Holds Us Together?

Session 3: On the Nature of Spirituality: What Is Holy?

Session 4: Sin and Salvation: Are We Saved?

Session 5: Eschatology: How Do We Account for Evil?

Session 6: Justice and the Beloved Community: What Is Our Place in the World?

Session 7: Individualism and Community: What Is the Role of the Liberal Church

Session 8: Suffering and Meaning: Why Do Bad Things Happen?

Session 9: Death and Immortality: How Do We Celebrate Life?

Session 10: A Spiritual Check-Up: Where Do We Go from Here?

Other